Wife Begins At Forty

A Comedy

Arne Sultan, Earl Barret
and Ray Cooney

Samuel French – London
New York – Sydney – Toronto – Hollywood

WIFE BEGINS AT FORTY

First presented, in association with the Theatre of
Comedy, at the Yvonne Arnaud Theatre, Guildford on
3rd September 1985.

Subsequently presented by the Theatre of Comedy
Company at the Ambassadors Theatre, London, on 1st
October 1985, with the following cast of characters:

Bernard Harper	Geoffrey Sumner
Gertie, the dog	Gertrude Bliss
George Harper	Dinsdale Landen
Linda Harper	Liza Goddard
Roger Dixon	John Quayle
Betty Dixon	Carol Hawkins
Leonard Harper	Stephen Leatherland

The play was directed by Ray Cooney
Designed by Saul Radomsky

In the Yvonne Arnaud Theatre production the part of
Betty Dixon was played by Yvonne D'Alpra

The action of the play takes place in the Harpers' living-
room in Woking, Surrey

ACT I Scene 1 The early hours of a Saturday morn-
ing in November
Scene 2 A week later. Early Friday evening
Scene 3 Noon the following day

ACT II Christmas Eve

Time—the present

ACT I

Scene 1

The living-room of the Harper home in Woking. 1.30 a.m. on a Saturday morning in November

The room has been quite tastefully decorated in a modern way. Everything blends in well with the exception of the curtains, which are too gaudy. Apart from the curtains, it is a typical upper middle class family home

In the L wall is a large fireplace with a settee in front of it and facing slightly out front. To the side of the fireplace is an electric fire. Downstage of the fireplace is a TV set facing upstage. Up C is the front door which leads out into an open porch. R of the front door is a door leading to a cloakroom. R of the cloakroom is a staircase leading up to the bedrooms. The wall R has large sliding windows which lead out on to an attractive patio. It is these windows which are covered by the gaudy curtains. Downstage of the windows is a door leading to the dining-room and the kitchen. Between the stairs and the sliding windows is a built-in drinks cabinet. There is a coffee table in front of the settee and DRC is a larger table to the right of which is a chair with arms. In the top left-hand corner of the room is a music centre and the telephone is on the drinks cabinet. There is a small table against the R end of the sofa and another chair against the wall to the left of the front door. There is a mirror on the wall DR. On the wall DL, above the TV is a framed picture of George and Linda (head and shoulders) in wedding regalia

When the CURTAIN rises, the window curtains are open. The room is dimly lit but the television set is switched on and a James Cagney film is the late night movie. Bernard Harper and Gertie, the dog, are sitting on the settee watching the film. Bernard is 75 years of age but very sprightly. Whilst keenly watching the film Bernard is feeding himself and Gertie potato crisps. Gertie can either be watching the movie or asleep depending on her mood. The remains of a fire is smouldering in the grate

The front door is opened and George Harper enters. George is in his mid-forties and ordinary but attractive. He is wearing wellington boots and his overcoat

Bernard continues to watch the TV. George switches the lights on

George (*as he enters*) Brr, it's cold. (*He sees Bernard*) Are you still up?

There is no reply from Bernard

Dad! I'm turning it down.

Bernard turns, gives a "salute" and returns to watching the TV. George goes over to the TV and turns the volume to a quieter level

It's half-past one. Dog shouldn't be on the sofa either.

There is no reply from Bernard. George goes to the cloakroom door, and starts to remove his overcoat

Bernard Have a good time tonight, son?

George (*removing his overcoat*) No, it was boring. (*He is revealed in his Superman costume. He looks out of the front door, as he removes his boots. Calling*) Linda! Come on darling! Stop messing about, you'll fall over the hedge. Oh, well if you want to catch cold, that's your problem. (*He gives up, and moves down to sit in the armchair*)

Linda "dances" in. She is wearing the costume of Wonderwoman. Linda is in her mid-thirties, very pretty and vivacious. She has a coat loosely over her costume

George lights his pipe

Linda (*as she enters, singing*) "I could have danced all night, I could have danced all night——"

George (*flatly*) You did. God, these evenings do go on. Come on, Gertie.

George sends Gertie off to the kitchen. Linda puts her coat in the cloakroom

Linda Ooh, I feel good. (*She sees Bernard*) Bernard, darling, you're still up. (*She gives him a hug*)

Bernard Ah! Good-evening, daughter-in-law.

George Good-*morning*, you mean.

Bernard What's that? Don't mumble, son.

Linda George says it's the morning.

Bernard Right, I'll put the kettle on.

Linda Lovely. Put the kettle on.

Linda helps Bernard out of the settee, and switches off the TV

George Don't bother.

Linda He's been waiting up for us, bless him. (*Louder, to Bernard*) Lovely. Cup of tea, O slave. (*She propels Bernard towards the kitchen*)

Bernard Three teas coming up from the Naafi.

George No tea for me. I'm going to bed.

Linda Oh no you're not. (*To Bernard*) Four cups, please, darling.

Bernard What's that?

Linda The Dixons are popping in for a nightcap.

Bernard Oh, not for me, thanks.

George (*moaning*) Oh.
Linda Roger and Betty from next door. Tea!
George Be quiet will you, you'll wake Leonard.
Bernard Why are you both dressed up like that?
Linda We're kinky!
George We've been to that blasted charity "do" at the Town Hall.
Bernard Oh. What are you supposed to be, son?

George gives Bernard a deadpan glare

George Superman!
Bernard Oh.
Linda And I'm Wonderwoman.
Bernard Well, at least one of you got it right.

Bernard exits, chuckling, into the kitchen

Linda goes to the record player and puts on a record

George He should be asleep at his age.
Linda Ah, he's a little sweetheart.
George We should all be in bed.
Linda Nonsense.

The music starts to play loudly. It is smoochy mood music

George Turn it down, will you? Leonard!

Linda turns it softer and dances sexily towards George

I don't know where you get your energy from.
Linda It must be my youth!
George Very funny!
Linda It's the wine. Wine always makes me feel alive, vital, exhilarated.
George (*yawning*) Yes me too.

Linda deposits herself on his lap

Careful!
Linda Sorry, Superman. (*Seductively*) Pity you invited Roger and Betty over.
George I didn't invite them. They invited themselves.
Linda Let's get rid of them as soon as we can.
George Yes, so we can get some sleep.
Linda Sleep isn't exactly what I had in mind, George.
George Linda!
Linda George!
George Please darling. I've got to get up in the morning.
Linda You could have a bit of a lie-in. It's Saturday.
George They expect me to be first in.
Linda You're the "boss man".
George That's all the more reason why I should be first in. Anyway, it's a very busy season for us.

George The dog shouldn't be——(*To Linda*) You'd better give him a hand with that toasting machine thing. You know what he's like, he'll electrocute himself.
Linda OK.
Betty I'll come with you. (*To Roger*) And don't you go without me.

Linda and Betty exit to the kitchen

Roger Well, how about that nightcap?
George Are you sure? We don't want to make you late.
Roger We haven't got far to stagger, have we? Only next door.
George (*rising, crossing to the bar*) I'll get you one, I've had enough.
Roger You didn't drink that much tonight.
George I had my limit. Two.
Roger Two? That won't even put a smile on your face.
George I don't like to exceed my limit. Don't like to lose control.
Roger That'll be the day.
George Besides, I don't fancy getting stopped by the police when I'm wearing something like this.
Roger Yes, not easy to give a sample with that lot on.
George (*admonishingly*) Roger!

Roger takes his drink from George. George turns the record player off

I hope this is the last year they have this silly Fancy Dress Ball.
Roger The Heart Disease Fund is a very good cause.
George That's what's so silly about it. Four hundred people smoking, drinking, eating, dancing. No wonder the heart attack rate goes up every year, it starts with this damn ball.
Roger So what, you only live once. Anyway, everybody there seemed to have a good time.
George Yes, especially you and that girl in the "Little Bo Peep" outfit. You spent half the night dancing with her.
Roger Yeah. She's a business acquaintance of mine.
George What, in your estate agency?
Roger Not exactly. She's a barmaid.
George You're an estate agent. How can a barmaid be a business acquaintance.
Roger She works in the pub around the corner from my office. She's more what you'd call an intimate friend.
George What's that mean?
Roger We're intimate every Monday and Wednesday night.
George What?!
Roger They're her nights off from the pub.
George (*stunned; blurting it out*) You're having an affair?
Roger Sshh! You'll wake Leonard.

George sits on the R end of the settee

George What do you tell Betty about Mondays and Wednesdays?

Roger I don't have to tell her anything. Monday's my snooker night and Wednesday's my poker night.

George Well, I'll say one thing. A rabbit is certainly the right costume for you. How long has this been going on?

Roger About a year.

George You've been seeing her for a year?

Roger Only on Mondays and Wednesdays. We use Sid Taylor's sailing boat.

George (*surprised*) Sid Taylor?

Roger Yes. You know, he's got this boat moored on the Thames.

George Sid Taylor lets you use his boat for that?

Roger Only on Mondays and Wednesdays. Sid and Judy go down there at weekends.

George Does Judy know?

Roger Not bloody likely.

George I can't believe Sid Taylor allows you to carry on like that on his boat. I thought he loved that boat.

Roger He does. How do you think he can afford to keep it without my twenty pounds a week rent?

George Roger, I have to tell you I'm shocked. I was always under the impression that you and Betty were happily married.

Roger We are. Betty and I have a terrific marriage.

George But you're deceiving her.

Roger That's what makes it so terrific! I'm a firm believer that fellows who have affairs make better husbands.

George And what about wives who have affairs?

Roger No, that'll ruin a marriage every time.

George reacts to this. He then moves to the bar to pour himself a Perrier water

George Well, I'm amazed that you jeopardize your marriage like this. I would never in a million years take a chance like that just for a few minutes in bed with some floozie.

Roger I wouldn't either for a few minutes, I make a whole evening of it! Raquel is insatiable.

George Raquel.

Roger My barmaid.

George You know your trouble, Roger? You place far too much emphasis on sex.

Roger And your problem is you place far too little emphasis on sex.

George What's that supposed to mean?

Roger George—if a marriage doesn't work in bed, it doesn't work at all.

George Well, my marriage works splendidly, thank you.

Roger Good.

George Linda and I have been married seventeen years. It's our *seventeenth anniversary* next week and I have everything I want right here. A wonderful wife, a fine son, a beautiful home, new carpets—new curtains! (*He pulls the curtains closed to show them off*) I'm a very happy man with a very happy marriage.

Roger What about your sex life!
George Fine!
Roger But does it work in bed?
George (*angrily*) Yes it does!
Roger Congratulations!
George (*angrily*) Thank you!

The front door opens and Leonard, the Harpers' sixteen-year-old son enters. He is a clean-cut, personable teenager. He is wearing an anorak

Leonard What's all the shouting about?
George We weren't shouting we were just—— (*Realizing*) I thought you were upstairs asleep. What are you doing out so late?
Leonard I went to a party at Geraldine's house. You knew I was going. Hello, Roger.
Roger Hi, Leonard.

Leonard puts his anorak in the cupboard

George And her parents let you children go on until one-thirty in the morning?
Leonard Her parents weren't there, they've gone to Torquay for the weekend.
George What kind of people are they to go away for the weekend and leave a sixteen-year-old girl at home all alone?
Leonard She wasn't alone, there were forty of us there.
George Go to bed, Leonard!
Leonard Good-night, Dad. Good-night, Roger.
Roger Good-night, Leonard.

Leonard exits up the stairs

There is a pause for a moment

Actually, my sex life has been really fantastic since the operation.
George Roger! I've heard quite enough about your vasectomy, thank you.
Roger It's done me the world of good.
George I'm sure it has.
Roger Yes. Just a little old "Snip, snip"——
George (*interrupting*) Roger, please!
Roger You should have it done, George.
George I don't want it done!
Roger Yes, terrific. Just a minor operation. Snip, snip, little knot, all over.
George (*sitting quickly*) Roger!! (*He sits on the R arm of the settee*)
Roger Means I don't have to worry about putting Betty in the pudding club. Or Raquel! I'll top myself up, shall I. (*He rises*)
George (*sighing*) If you must.

Roger does so

Roger Yes. I was telling the fellows at the golf club about the advantages of my vasectomy.

George Honestly, Roger, I don't know how you can go about broadcasting it like that.
Roger It's nothing to have it done these days. The women appreciate it too. No messing about with pills. Or contraceptives.
George Roger!

Roger returns to sit on the L *end of the settee*

Roger I bet your sex life would improve no end.
George (*tersely*) There's nothing wrong with my sex life.
Roger How often then?
George Roger, really!
Roger Weekly?
George Please!
Roger Oh dear, quarterly.
George Look, I don't do it to a timetable.

Roger sips his drink

Roger What safety measures do you and Linda use?

George rises angrily

George Roger, I don't want to discuss it!
Roger Oh, you're very uptight about it George. Take my advice. Have a vasectomy. I was in and out in half an hour.
George It's not my cup of tea at all.
Roger God, you're a stick in the mud.
George (*angrily*) Just because you don't want to get your barmaid pregnant you think a crafty snip-snip——

Linda and Betty appear in the kitchen doorway carrying a tray with mugs of tea

(*Continuing without missing a beat*)—I think it's a big mistake for the Government to sell arms to either side in the Middle East.

George moves behind the settee to DL, *glaring at Roger who is grinning*

Betty Now that's enough politics, George.

Betty sits on the R *end of the settee. Linda sits on the armchair*

Roger Yes, you're right. Change the subject, George.

Bernard enters with two toasted sandwiches on plates. Gertie follows him on

Bernard Toasted sandwiches coming up. How's that for speed?
Roger Excellent service.

Bernard starts to feed the dog

George You mustn't give the dog toasted sandwiches.
Bernard It's her first today.
George She shouldn't be eating bread at all.

Betty Yes, he became quite distant. And I came to the conclusion that we
were spending too much time together. Like you just said, we weren't
"communicating", just spending time together.
Linda So what did you do?
Betty I suggested that he got out of the house. So he started playing
snooker on Monday nights and poker on Wednesday nights.
Linda Snooker and poker.
Betty And I must say he became a changed man! Your George doesn't have
any hobbies, does he?
Linda No, nothing.

Betty rises and collects her coat

Betty That's probably all that's wrong. Now, I think it's very important
you and George sit down and discuss this, so lock yourselves in the loo if
you have to.
Linda Thanks.

Linda gives Betty her basket

Bernard comes in with Gertie

Bernard It's a lovely night out there. Frost in the morning, though.
Linda Come on, Gertie!

Linda takes Gertie off into the kitchen

Bernard You off, Mrs D?
Betty Yes.
Bernard Might see you in the garden tomorrow . . .
Betty You bet. What's on your agenda?
Bernard Well now. Roses get their autumn pruning but the first priority is
the lawn. Winter dressing.
Betty You spoil that lawn, Bernard.
Bernard Lawns are like women my dear—treat them lovingly and they'll let
you walk all over them.

Betty chuckles and gives him a hug

Betty You're a wicked old chauvinist.
Bernard Yes. It's got me everywhere.

Betty laughs and exits through the front door

Linda returns from the kitchen

Hey! Where's your smile?
Linda Gone on holiday.
Bernard Bit early. Christmas is a few weeks away yet.
Linda (*laughing*) Fool!
Bernard Well, I'm off to bed.
Linda 'Night, Dad.
Bernard Sleep tight. (*He goes to the stairs but stops*) It was easier when the
war was on. Not so much danger about today. Makes some of you feel the

need to manufacture excitement. Not easy today, sweetheart. (*He starts to go upstairs*)

George comes downstairs, half out of his Superman costume, pyjama jacket in hand, wearing his pyjama trousers

George Darling, I've got something caught in my zip.
Bernard That sounds painful.
George Bed!

Bernard exits upstairs

Linda assists George out of costume, and he puts his pyjama jacket on

Maybe we should give the ball a miss next year.
Linda If you say so, darling. (*During the following speech, she hangs George's costume in the cloakroom and returns to him*)
George Bit difficult though, I suppose—to give it a miss. We'd be missed. We ought to be seen, I think. Good for us we get involved with the social life of Woking. Especially if I'm going to stand for the local council. Yes, do my bit for the local community. Better not give it a miss.
Linda George?
George Mm?
Linda Can we talk?
George I've just been talking . . .

Linda moves to the settee

Linda It's important. Very important.
George Can't it wait till morning?
Linda I don't think so.

Linda sits on the L end of the settee. George sighs, crosses to the settee and sits down beside Linda

George What is it?
Linda George . . . how do you feel about snooker?
George (*a beat, then he rises*) Good-night, Linda. (*He moves to go*)
Linda George! I want you to start playing snooker on Monday nights with Roger.

George takes this in

George Linda, the way Roger plays snooker, I don't think he'd care for company. Besides, I don't need snooker, I'm very happy, dear.
Linda Well, I'm not.
George All right, then you go and play snooker. (*He moves to the stairs*)
Linda George, please! I believe snooker could help.
George (*stunned, starting back towards her*) Linda, you and I have been married all these years, I had no idea you were so keen on snooker. (*He sits beside her on the settee*)
Linda Help our marriage!
George What's snooker got to do with our marriage?

Linda George, it's not working.
George What isn't?
Linda Our marriage!
George What the hell happened? It was working five minutes ago when I went up to bed.
Linda George. Dear George—living with you is like living with a machine.
George (*blankly*) A machine.
Linda You get up in the morning, go to work, come home, go to sleep, get up in the morning and go to work again.
George Yes, I know I do.
Linda Every day.
George That's right.
Linda George, you're not alive. In seventeen years you haven't grown.
George How can you sit there and say I haven't grown? Fifteen years ago when I went into the artificial flower business Barclays Bank gave me an overdraft facility of twenty-five thousand pounds. Today I have three shops—one in Woking, one in Epsom and one in East Grinstead—all doing well. And now I have an overdraft with Barclays of two hundred thousand pounds. Don't tell me that isn't growing.

Linda rises in exasperation and moves in front of the settee to c

Linda When I talk about growing, I mean "living". Expanding our horizons. DOING things. (*She turns to him*) Together. Having fun. Don't go into the shop tomorrow. Take the day off. Take the whole of next week off.
George We're stock-taking next week.

Linda kneels beside the R *end of the settee*

Linda George! Do something crazy!
George I think maybe I did, seventeen years ago.
Linda (*rising*) I can't even talk to you.

George pulls her down on to the settee

George Because there's really nothing to talk about. You're just a bit sloshed tonight, Linda, and you're being irrational. So far you haven't mentioned one valid thing that's wrong with our marriage.

Linda looks at him for a moment

Linda Sex.
George Sex.
Linda S-E-X.
George (*rising*) Oh! Oh, I see! That's what this is all about! We haven't been getting our rations! Right! We'll do something about that right away. Let's talk!

George sits beside her again and she rises

Linda (*angrily*) I'm going to bed!
George Well, I'll be up in a couple of minutes so put on a very sexy nightie.

Linda stops and turns

Linda All right, George, I will.

Linda exits up the stairs

George (*calling upstairs*) On second thoughts don't bother with the nightie at all! (*He smiles to himself*) Ahh! (*He looks at his watch*) Oh God! (*He decides he needs a brandy so pours himself a large one*) Good luck George. (*He drinks the brandy, and turns the various lights out, while muttering about his Saturday schedule*) I've got to be in Woking at eight-fifteen ... East Grinstead at nine ... Very busy day. God! Bloody sandwiches all over the place. My father's turning the house into a Naafi! (*He takes the plate towards the kitchen*)

Gertie comes out

Gertie! You should be in your basket. Oh, all right.

George sits on the sofa, and Gertie sits in front of him. He feeds Gertie the remains of the sandwich

I don't understand you women at all, Gertie. Absolute mystery. You work sixteen hours a day to give them everything they've been asking for and they're still not happy. Beautiful home, lovely furniture, carpets, curtains, car—two cars ... lovely son ... lovely dog. Not enough. She wants sex at two o'clock in the morning. All right. She wants sex, she'll get sex. I'll go up there and give her such sex she won't bother me again till Christmas nineteen ninety-nine.

George rests his head on this hands. After a moment, Linda's voice can be heard from, upstairs

Linda (*off*) George? George?

George emits a snore

George?

Gertie exits upstairs as——

Black-out

SCENE 2

The same. Early Friday evening. A week later

Some of the lights are on. The windows are closed but the curtains are open

Linda, wearing a very chic party dress, comes downstairs. She goes out of the front door and stands in the porch looking down the street

Betty comes downstairs, also wearing a party dress. Betty is fixing her hair as she speaks

Betty Any sign of him? (*She goes to the mirror* DR)
Linda No.
Betty Surely he won't be late for your anniversary?

Linda closes the door and moves DC

Linda I'm getting worried. I called the shop and the manager said he left hours ago.
Betty Maybe he's at one of the other shops.
Linda No, I've checked.

Betty moves to Linda at C

Betty Probably stopped off at the pub.
Linda George? He wouldn't do anything that daring.
Betty You're sure he doesn't suspect that you want to leave him?
Linda I only made up my mind last night. I haven't said a word to George yet. I didn't want to spoil today with it being our anniversary.
Betty So when will you tell him?
Linda Tomorrow.

Linda goes to the front door again. Betty moves behind the settee

Betty You'll have changed your mind by tomorrow.
Linda No I won't. I'm going.
Betty It'll shake George rigid.
Linda I know.

Betty sits on the L *arm of the settee*

Betty I should've cancelled this anniversary party Roger and I are giving for you tonight.
Linda No, it'll do George good to have a party.
Betty There's going to be thirty old friends toasting the happy couple.
Linda I know.
Betty And thirty anniversary presents.
Linda I know!
Betty Well, don't unwrap them then they'll be easier to send back.

Bernard comes downstairs wearing an old-fashioned dinner jacket. It just about fits him and at the moment he is minus his tie

Bernard Has the anniversary boy arrived?
Betty Not yet.

Linda brings him DC, *coming to his* R

Linda But don't forget: Betty's party's a surprise. George thinks he and I are having a quiet little supper at home, just the two of us.
Bernard Of course. Mum's the word.
Linda So don't let him see you all dressed up in a dinner jacket.
Bernard Having a spot of bother with my collar stud actually.

Betty moves to Bernard's L

Betty You look ravishing.
Bernard (*tapping his jacket*) Oh, thank you. Nineteen forty-nine. Still fits me like a glove.
Betty Marvellous.
Linda He's a fibber. He's had it let out half-a-dozen times at least.
Bernard All right! Haven't had to touch the sleeves, though, have I? Exciting, isn't it? I love parties. Did I ever tell you girls how Jumbo Phillpots and I celebrated VE Day?
Linda Yes. You and Jumbo Phillpots drank so much champagne——
Betty —you were drunk for a week.
Bernard Certainly not. It was a month actually.
Betty Go and put your tie on.
Linda And if George sees you in your dinner jacket just say you're going to the theatre.
Bernard Theatre?
Linda You're seeing *Cats*.
Bernard Cats?
Betty It's a musical.
Bernard Musical cats?

The girls push him upstairs

Linda Never mind. Go and finish dressing.
Bernard Musical cats?
Betty (*calling*) Don't forget—you're looking for your tie.
Bernard (*as he goes*) Tie? Cats? Musical?

Bernard exits upstairs

Betty (*to Linda*) Have you considered Bernard?
Linda Bernard?
Betty If you and George split, who'll get custody of him?
Linda I can't let George's father govern my life, can I?
Betty And there's Leonard.
Linda Yes—there's Leonard. And the dog.

The telephone rings. Linda answers it

(*On the phone*) Hello? . . . OK Roger, she'll be right there. (*She hangs up*) Some of the guests have arrived.
Betty (*hurrying to the front door*) I'll see you in a minute. God, I feel nervous. I wish you hadn't told me about you and George, you've set my relaxation classes back about twelve months. (*She opens the front door and closes it*) It's George! He's just getting out of his car.
Linda Thank goodness for that. You go out the back way. If he sees the pair of us dressed like this even George might suspect it's more than just a quiet supper at home. (*She opens the sliding windows*)
Betty I've never felt so nervous in all my life. I don't know how I'll be able to talk to George tonight.
Linda Don't worry, there'll be thirty other people over there.
Betty God, it's like a celebration before the execution.

Betty exits on to the patio

Linda adjusts her ear-rings in the mirror

The front door opens and George is framed in the doorway, with a broad smile on his face. He is carrying his briefcase and an umbrella and wearing his trilby hat and overcoat. He closes the door

Linda (*her back to him*) George, where have you been? I called the shop and they said you left hours ago.
George (*grinning happily*) Yes.
Linda Well, why are you so late?
George Do you think I could have a drink?
Linda Why are you standing there like that?
George Where I've been is why I'm standing here like this.
Linda What on earth are you talking about?
George Do you think you could get me a drink?

Linda eyes him and then goes to the cabinet and pours him a whisky and water while George, unnoticed by Linda, hobbles cheerfully into the room, using his umbrella as a walking stick

Linda Have you had an accident in the car?
George (*smiling*) No.
Linda Well what is it for heaven's sake?
George (*very pleased with himself*) I've been to see Doctor James.
Linda Doctor who? What's happened? Are you all right?
George I am now!
Linda I've never heard you mention Doctor James, I didn't even know you were ill.
George I'm not. Doctor James is a urologist.
Linda Is that ears, nose and throat?

George smiles and shakes his head

George (*proudly*) I've had a vasectomy.
Linda (*blankly*) Vasectomy.
George Yes. (*He kisses Linda's forehead and takes his drink*)
Linda (*stunned*) Oh, my God. (*She pours herself a brandy*)
George Linda, is that sofa on castors?
Linda Mm? No.
George Then I'll have to keep going. (*He continues behind the settee and takes off his hat and coat, placing them on the back of the settee*)
Linda (*upset*) George, how could you go and have a vasectomy just like that? And why did you pick today of all days?
George Because today's our wedding anniversary.
Linda What's our anniversary got to do with it?
George I wanted to give you a present. Only you can't actually have it for ten days. (*He lowers himself on to the settee and sips his drink*)
Linda Oh, George! (*She moves DR and sits in the armchair*)
George What is it?

Linda You shouldn't have done it.

George Nothing to get upset about. You *are* a soppy thing. You're just the same when we have it done to the cats.

Linda It isn't that, it's——(*She stops, near to tears*)

George What?

Linda You shouldn't have had it done.

They both drink

George Why are you all dressed up? I thought we were having a quiet evening at home.

Linda Betty and George invited us over to their place for an anniversary drink.

George You better tell them I can't make it. Ask them to come over here.

Linda (*her voice rising*) They can't come here.

George Why not?

Linda They've got thirty people over there!

George Thirty people——?!

Linda It's a surprise party for us. I didn't want to tell you!

George (*angrily*) You know I hate surprise parties.

Linda (*angrily*) That's why I didn't want to tell you.

George Well, we're not going!

Linda We'll have to! We can't spoil the surprise for all those people.

George What surprise? Everybody knew about it except me.

Linda George——!

George Now *I* know it so there's no surprise.

Linda rises furiously and moves C

Linda (*shouting*) Betty's been planning this bloody party for three weeks!

George Linda!

Linda Three weeks!

George Linda, don't shout. The one thing Doctor James said was "No shouting".

Linda (*shouting*) That was for you, not for me!

George It doesn't matter. When you shout, it hurts.

He indicates his lap. Linda marches UL

Linda The guests are already there!

George Could you get me some ice please!

Linda comes DL

Linda You don't usually have ice in your drinks.

George Ice for an ice-bag.

Linda You haven't got a headache as well, have you?

George When you've had what I've had it's not your head that aches. Doctor James told me ice would help.

Linda (*angrily*) You shouldn't have had it done in the first place!

George And it would show a little more sympathy if you just got me some ice.

Linda marches in front of him

Linda All right. How would you like it, in cubes or in balls?

Linda exits furiously into the kitchen

George (*shouting after her*) Charming! (*Reminding himself*) Don't shout.

Bernard enters from upstairs trying to tie his bow tie. He comes DC

Bernard I thought I heard you.
George Oh, hello, Dad.
Bernard Can you tie a bow tie?
George Yes. Of course I can tie a bow tie.
Bernard Good. Education wasn't totally wasted then.

George rises and joins Bernard. During the ensuing dialogue, George ties Bernard's tie

(*Over-casual*) If you're wondering why I'm all dressed up—I'm going to the cinema.
George (*surprised*) You're going to the cinema in a dinner jacket?
Bernard Yes. I'm going to see *Puss in Boots*.

George tries to take this in but gives up

George God, you're eccentric.
Bernard No, not really. Now, Jock McIntosh was eccentric. Pilot "A" Squadron.
George Yes, Dad. I know all about Jock McIntosh.
Bernard Insisted on flying in a kilt. Good luck omen. Shot down in Occupied France, October nineteen forty-two. Kilt saved his bacon!
George Operated as a parachute, I suppose.
Bernard (*chuckling*) That's very funny, George. Why aren't you laughing?
George I'm not allowed to laugh.
Bernard Why not?
George I told you I was going to see Doctor James.
Bernard Oh, that's right! You've had a lobotomy.

George reacts and sits on the settee

George Go to the cinema!
Bernard Cinema!
George You're going to the cinema, aren't you?
Bernard Why, what's on?
George I don't know.
Bernard Anyway, I can't go to the cinema. I'm going to your surprise anniversary party.
George (*realizing*) Oh. So that's why you're all dressed up?
Bernard Why else would I dress up? I worry about you sometimes, George.
(*He wanders towards the stairs*)

Leonard comes in, wearing football gear and looking very muddy

Leonard (*shouting from the front door as he enters*) Mum, I'm home! (*Seeing Bernard*) Hi, Grandad.

Leonard throws Bernard the ball

Bernard Hello there, Leonard. Did you win?
Leonard You bet! Five-one.

Bernard throws the ball back

Bernard Well done. Wonderful sport, rugger.

Bernard exits upstairs

Leonard sees George lying on the sofa

Leonard Hello, Dad.
George (*weakly*) Hello, son.
Leonard Everything OK?
George Well to tell you the truth, I'm not feeling too——
Leonard Hey!
George Yes?
Leonard Do you know how many goals I scored today?
George No.
Leonard Two.
George (*weakly*) Well done.
Leonard One left-footer from thirty yards and one fantastic header—booph! (*He heads the ball fiercely into George's vasectomy*)
George (*yelling with pain*) Ahhh!
Leonard Good save, Dad. (*He takes the ball back*)

The dining-room door opens and Linda appears with the ice-bag

Linda Did you call George?
George (*mumbling with pain*) Oo—in—ah—oh . . .
Linda Do talk sense George. Leonard, go and have a bath.
Leonard OK.

Leonard exits upstairs with the ball

Linda Here's your ice-bag.

She tosses the ice-bag to George. Before he can intercept it, it lands on his vasectomy. He reacts with a silent scream

Oh, I'm sorry, dear.
George And for the next ten days no throwing, just handing.
Linda (*sympathetically*) Yes, I'm sorry. I really am. And I'm sorry I shouted at you just now.
George I'm sorry I shouted, too. And we'll go to the party. Roger and Betty must have been to a lot of trouble.
Linda Are you sure you're feeling all right?
George (*smiling*) I think so.

Linda sits on the R arm of the settee

Linda Oh George, I do wish you hadn't had it done.
George I did it for us.
Linda Well, you shouldn't have!
George So that when we want to make love we can just go ahead and do it.

Linda rises trying to hide her emotions

Linda Roger and Betty are waiting for us.

George pulls her down on to the settee

George Before we go, I've got something for you. (*He takes two ring boxes from his pocket*)
Linda What is it?
George It's the rest of our anniversary present. New wedding rings for both of us. (*He places the boxes on the table*)
Linda Oh, George.
George Well, it's been seventeen years. The inscription on my old one is so worn out I can hardly read it. (*He removes his gold ring*) My "L"s have completely gone. (*He strains to read the inside of his ring*) "To George ... with 'ove—'inda". How's yours?

Linda removes her gold ring and looks at it

Linda My "D"s have gone. (*She reads*) "To my 'earest 'ear".
George (*handing her her box*) There we are, my 'earest 'ear.

Linda removes the ring from the box

Linda (*quietly*) Thank you George. "Seventeen years and still my dearest". It's beautiful. But you shouldn't have done it.
George You always say that. For seventeen years. Every time I buy you something you say "You shouldn't have done it".
Linda (*near to tears*) This time I'm saying it for a different reason. (*She hands the ring back*) I can't take it.
George (*chuckling*) Linda, if you're worried because you haven't got a surprise for me——
Linda (*rising*) George, please! Roger and Betty are waiting for us. (*She moves to pick up her handbag*)
George Linda! Why can't you take it?
Linda George, this isn't the time.
George Linda!

Linda hesitates, in a turmoil

Linda All right, George. (*She takes a deep breath*) George—I want us to separate.

George looks blank as he tries to take this in. He then looks down at his vasectomy. He then places the ice-bag on his head. He then laughs. This hurts so he replaces the ice-bag on his vasectomy. Linda breaks DR

A trial separation. I hadn't planned to tell you today. I didn't want to spoil our anniversary. George, try to understand. I'm NOT happy with my life any more.

Linda sits in the armchair. George rises and hobbles towards her clutching the ice-bag

George That's the most ridiculous thing I ever heard. You must be happy. I'm happy.
Linda No, George, you're not happy either.
George I am! I'm bloody happy!
Linda (*shaking her head*) No, George, you only think you're happy.
George (*shouting*) Don't tell me I only think I'm happy—I'm happy, for God's sake. Look at me! (*He leans across the table and thrusts an angry face at Linda*) Isn't this the face of a happy man?
Linda (*tearfully*) George, it's our marriage. It's stifling me.

Linda rises and moves in front of George to pick up her handkerchief. George hobbles painfully after her

George When did you decide about this?
Linda It's been something that's been building up inside me for some time. I tried to tell you last week after the dance, but, well I finally decided last night.
George Last night.
Linda In bed.

George takes this in

George We made love last night, didn't we?
Linda Yes.
George Well, did you make the decision before or after?
Linda During.

George digests this

George (*suddenly angry*) How the blazes could you think about us separating while I was doing that?
Linda (*her voice rising*) You weren't doing anything, George. You fell asleep on top of me.
George (*trying to recall*) Did I do that again?
Linda Yes, you did that again. (*She turns and walks away*)
George (*hobbling after her*) Linda, this will kill me.
Linda I'm sorry, George. You forced me to tell you.
George No, it's not the telling—it's the walking. (*He shouts*) Stand still!

Linda stops and turns. They are now face to face

All right. Now—tell me. I can take it. Who is he?
Linda What do you mean?
George The other man.
Linda There's no other man, dear.

George sits her in the armchair

George Don't be ridiculous. You don't just decide to end seventeen years of happily married life unless there's another man.

Linda George, it's our marriage. We don't have anything anymore.

George moves around the room

George How can you say that? Just look around you. We have this gorgeous house, brand new carpets, new curtains . . . (*He pulls the curtains across the windows*)

Linda George, I don't want to hear about the carpets and the curtains any more. I hate the curtains!

George is dumbfounded

George (*blankly*) You hate the curtains! I got a very good reduction on these curtains.

Linda I loathe them!

George I didn't know you felt that way about the curtains. We've had them for six months, you never said anything before.

Leonard comes down the stairs dressed to go out. He goes towards the front door

Leonard See you, Mum. See you, Dad.

Linda Where're you going, Leonard?

Leonard Down the disco.

Linda Don't you have any homework?

Leonard Did it at school. See you. (*He moves to go*)

Linda Don't lock up when you get back. We'll probably be late.

Leonard OK. Have fun. (*He moves to go*)

George Leonard.

Leonard (*stopping*) Yes?

George Come over here, son.

Leonard (*crossing, apprehensively*) Anything wrong?

George No, I just want your opinion about something. Do you like the curtains?

Leonard (*enthusiastically*) Fantastic.

George (*to Linda, vindicated*) Did you hear that?

Leonard When did you get them?

George (*annoyed*) Good-night, Leonard.

Leonard exits through the front door

Leonard likes the curtains.

Linda The curtains aren't important. I'm not talking about materialistic things. I'm talking about our marriage——

George moves down to her

George Linda, our marriage is going to be OK now.

Linda Improving our sex life isn't the answer.

George You said it was.

Linda rises, confused

Linda It's not the whole answer. It's difficult to say whether it's forty per cent of this and thirty-five per cent of that or eighty per cent of that and fifteen per cent of this.

George Darling, neither of those add up to a hundred . . .

Linda moves in front of him to the settee

Linda George, it's us. You and me. What we are. I know I'm far from perfect. (*She sits on the* L *end of the settee*)

George (*moving to Linda*) I thought you'd never mention it. It's all very well going on about me. What about you? Any time a problem comes up you never think about it rationally. You never discuss it sensibly. You just meet it head on, and make a decision, right or wrong.

Linda That's not true.

George Yes, it is. You're doing it right now with all this talk about separating. It's crazy. (*He sits beside Linda*)

Linda George, I know you're hurt. I know you're confused and I understand that.

George *I'm* confused!

Linda You see, George, I was so busy being caught up in your life that I stopped having one of my own. And that's what I want now. Roger and Betty will be wondering what's happened to us. I'll get my coat.

Linda rises and goes into the cloakroom. George sighs then decides to put on a brave front

George (*calling out*) All right, Linda, we won't discuss it any more tonight. We'll go to the party as though nothing's happened. Have a good time. Right, dear?

Linda comes out of the cloakroom wearing her coat and moves DC

Linda Right, dear.

George rises and moves to Linda at C

George Linda . . .

Linda Yes?

George Who is he?

Linda George, there is no other man. There's never been another man in my life and you've got to believe that. I mean, I believe you when you tell me there's never been another woman in your life.

George (*too quickly*) Right, let's go. (*He turns away and moves to collect his hat and coat from the settee*)

Linda Well, has there?

George What?

Linda moves up to the R *end of the settee*

Linda Been another woman in your life?

George (*looking at his watch*) We've got to go. (*He comes* DL *and moves to* DC)

Linda (*warningly*) George. (*She moves* DC *to George's* R)

George Before we were married there were several women in my life.

Linda I mean, since we've been married.

George This is a fine time to start asking bloody silly questions like this.

Linda Has there?

George (*after a pause*) One.

Linda is very surprised

Linda (*hurt*) George.

George Only one in *seventeen years*.

Linda When did it happen?

George puts on his hat and coat

George Come on darling——

Linda George!

George Look, we've got to go——

Linda George!

George Darling, please——

Linda When did it happen?!

George On our honeymoon.

Linda (*amazed*) You were unfaithful on our honeymoon? In Torremolinos?

George Yes.

Linda Where was I, for heaven's sake?

George You were in bed.

Linda In bed?

George If you remember you were in bed for three days. Spanish tummy.

Linda Oh, yes.

George You just lay there for three whole days—just moaning and groaning. Anyway after a couple of days sitting in my room and twiddling my thumbs I thought I'd go down to the bar for a drink.

Linda And?

George She was sitting at the bar.

Linda She?

George The flamenco dancer.

Linda Flamenco dancer?

George Yes.

Linda I see. So you decided to have an affair right there and then.

George No. She was between shows and we just struck up a conversation.

Linda I didn't realize your Spanish was so hot.

George It isn't. She spoke jolly good English. She was from Wigan, actually.

Linda (*deadpan*) Wigan?

George Yes. Well we had a few drinks and then she suggested we take a stroll.

Linda (*brightly brittle*) A stroll?

George Yes. On the beach.

Linda (*with feigned delight*) On the beach?
George (*chuckling*) And she started to teach me the flamenco.
Linda (*chuckling icily*) She didn't!
George (*laughing*) Yes. You know the old . . . (*He mimes the flamenco*) Well, of course, we fell over!
Linda You didn't!
George Yes, we did! There we were rolling all over the beach.
Linda You weren't?!
George Yes, we were! You would have laughed, darling.
Linda Oh I would, darling!

They are both now laughing but George still doesn't see the murder in Linda's merriment. George's laughter gradually subsides

George Well, I don't know if it was the alcohol or the moonlight or what but before I knew it——
Linda You were at it on the beach.
George Yes. Well, half on the beach. Our feet were in the water. You know, like "From Here to Eternity". (*Chuckling*) Oh, I wish you'd been there.

Linda manages to refrain from throttling him but grits her teeth and then moves up to the stairs as George opens the front door for her

Linda (*calling upstairs*) Bernard! Bernard! Come on, we're off!
Bernard (*off*) Receiving you loud and clear.
Linda (*to George*) See you at the party. Olé!

Linda does a quick foot-stamping and a flamenco gesture and exits

Bernard comes downstairs wearing his RAF greatcoat and white silk scarf

Bernard Roger, Wilco and chocks away!
George Dad?
Bernard Yes, son?
George What's your opinion of those curtains?
Bernard The curtains?
George Yes, what do you think?
Bernard (*shrugging*) They're curtains.
George They don't actually offend you?
Bernard The curtains.
George Yes.
Bernard Offend me.
George Yes.
Bernard No. Take more than a bloody awful pair of curtains like that to offend me.

Bernard exits

George looks sadly at the curtains and then follows Bernard out, closing the door

Black-out

SCENE 3

The same. It is noon the following day

Winter sunshine streams in through the open sliding windows, but the fire is flickering in the fireplace. A wheelbarrow stands inside the patio doors, full of weeds and bush prunings

Leonard and Gertie are sitting on the sofa with a tray full of snacks, while watching the television. An excited commentator is reporting an international football match between England and Ireland. Leonard gives Gertie one of the sausage rolls. They concentrate on the TV

After a moment George comes downstairs in pyjamas and dressing gown, carrying a glass of fizzing Alka Seltzer. He has a dreadful hangover

George (*seeing the wheelbarrow*) God! (*Calling off*) Dad! Dad!

George gets no reply. He moves to the TV and switches it off

Leonard Hey, what did you do that for?
George Gertie, off there! (*He sends Gertie out*)

Gertie exits

I want to have a little talk, Leonard.
Leonard That's Grandstand.
George This is much more important than Grandstand.
Leonard Oh, not now, Dad. They're showing highlights from last Wednes-
day's international soccer match.
George Leonard what I want to talk to you about——

Bernard enters from the patio, carrying a rake

Bernard Someone left this rake in the middle of the lawn——

George moves angrily to Bernard

George Dad, will you leave us alone please? Go and weed in the garden.
Bernard Do what?
George Weed!
Bernard Oh. For a moment I thought you said—never mind. (*He chuckles*)
George Dad, please! Now, Leonard——
Bernard Someone left this rake in the middle of the lawn. That's very
dangerous. Dickie Price trod on a rake once—smack!
George Dad! It makes no difference to me whether Dickie Price trod on a
rake or whether he didn't tread on a rake.
Bernard It made a difference to Dickie Price, I can tell you.

Bernard exits with the wheelbarrow and the rake

Leonard Can I watch the soccer now, Dad?

George Leonard, what I want to say is more important than soccer. It concerns your life. In fact it concerns more than your life—it concerns your future.

Leonard (*seriously*) It's as important as that, is it, Dad?

George Yes.

Leonard OK. I'll switch the set on but turn the volume down. (*He does so. Settling back in the settee*) OK Dad. Fire away.

George Leonard, your mother and I have been married for seventeen years now and for the most part it's been a very good marriage. A very good marriage. Wouldn't you say this has been a happy home, son?

Leonard Dreadful!

George Mm?

Leonard No wonder Arsenal sold him.

George moves around the room as he talks

George As I was saying. We as a family have everything that anybody could possibly want. (*He indicates*) A beautiful home—new carpets—new curtains——

Leonard Dad.

George Yes?

Leonard Is this about you and Mum separating?

George (*surprised*) Yes.

Leonard Oh.

George Who told you?

Leonard You did.

George Did I? When?

Leonard Last night. When you got home from the party?

George I spoke to you last night?

Leonard (*nodding*) Don't you remember?

George (*thinking*) I don't think so.

Leonard You came into my room at three o'clock this morning and told me all about the separation and how you'd decided it was best for *you* to be the one to move out.

George At three o'clock in the morning I woke you up and told you all that? The separation. Me moving out.

Leonard Yes. And about the flamenco dancer.

George (*shocked*) I didn't tell you about the flamenco dancer?

Leonard Don't you remember?

George shakes his head and sits on the R end of the settee

Do you remember falling down the stairs?

George I told you about falling down the stairs at the party?

Leonard No, you fell down the stairs when you left my room.

George Good God, I fell down the stairs here, as well, did I? No wonder my vasectomy doesn't hurt any more, I'm probably paralysed from the waist down. You know son, you haven't told me how you feel about it.

Leonard Well, England's got a good team now, but if Ireland——

George rises

George (*interrupting*) I'm not talking about football! I'm talking about your mother and me separating. Me leaving home.
Leonard Oh.

George leans over Leonard and places his hand on his shoulder warmly

George Come on, son. Don't hold anything back. Tell me how you feel about it.
Leonard (*casually*) Fine.
George (*dumbly*) Fine?

Leonard nods. George moves to C *to look at Leonard*

That's an answer? Fine?
Leonard Dad, if you and Mother aren't happy together, why hang in there?
George I beg your pardon?
Leonard Why keep going? I mean, you're two mature people. It's been OK in the past. You've been wonderful parents but now you should do what's best for yourself—split.
George (*angrily*) What kind of a bloody attitude is that?
Leonard You asked me how I felt.
George (*shouting*) I didn't know you felt like that, you callous young swine.
Leonard Take it easy——
George Your parents are ending seventeen years of married bliss, son!
Leonard Well, if it's bliss, why——
George Shut up! Seventeen years of married bliss and all you can say is "Yeah, that's fine, split"! You're our only son. I'm leaving home. It's got to affect you more than that. (*He moves upstage, distressed*)
Leonard Well, of course——

George comes back to behind Leonard

George That's more like it. Go on, son, tell me. (*He puts his hands on Leonard's shoulders*)
Leonard Well, first of all, Mum's going to have to collect me from parties, and her driving scares the hell out of me.

George turns Leonard's head towards the TV

George You watch your football. (*He sadly moves towards the stairs*)
Leonard OK Dad. But if you come back at half-time I wouldn't mind hearing about the flamenco dancer again.

George throws his arms in the air and moves towards the stairs. Leonard turns up the volume on the TV as:

> *Linda enters from the front door carrying two shopping bags of groceries. She is wearing a coat and is visibly upset. She walks straight past George, ignoring him and puts one shopping bag by the table next to the armchair* DR

George Hello, dear!
Linda (*tersely*) You got up then.

George moves to Linda

George I wouldn't mind a cup of coffee or——

Linda moves in front of George to the settee

Linda (*interrupting*) Leonard, will you switch that off and watch it in your room. I want to talk to your father.

Leonard My old set's no good. I want to watch it in colour.

George Are you all right, dear?

Linda (*furiously*) Your behaviour at the party last night was absolutely disgusting!

Leonard (*grabbing his tray*) Black and white will be fine.

Leonard rushes upstairs

Linda moves DL *and switches off the TV, leaving the second shopping bag by the TV*

Linda (*as she moves*) In all the years we've been married I've never seen you drink so much.

George I've never had such a good reason.

Linda Our problems are between you and me. You had no right telling everybody at the party.

George I didn't tell everyone.

Linda No, you didn't just tell them—you announced it. From the top of Betty's piano.

George Betty's piano.

Linda You got up on the piano and announced—having got absolute silence—that our marriage was over and that you were moving out.

George (*befuddled*) I have no recollection of that at all.

Linda sits on the L *end of the settee*

Linda It was awful. George, I will never forgive you for humiliating me in front of our friends.

George Well, what's the difference? They would have found out sooner or later.

Linda About the separation yes. They need never have known about the flamenco dancer.

George shocked, sits on the R *end of the settee*

George I didn't tell them about the flamenco dancer?

Linda In detail.

George Oh, God!

Linda You gave an appalling impersonation of the pair of you groaning and rolling all over the beach.

George Linda, dear——(*He places his hand on her arm*)

Linda Don't you "dear" me! (*She rises and breaks to* C)

George I was so unhappy.

Linda The thirty other guests weren't. They were hysterical. Especially when you started telling jokes about your vasectomy.

George Oh, no!

Linda "New balls please"! (*She furiously moves to cloakroom and hangs up her coat*)

George I'd had one hell of a day. The operation. You saying what you did right out of the blue like that. Linda, let's talk.

Linda George, it's too late. I've been wanting to talk for seventeen years.

George I just can't believe it.

Linda looks upstairs

Linda George, we're going to have to tell Leonard about us.

George He—er—already knows. I had a talk with him before you came in.

Linda (*moving* DC) Poor baby. How did he take it?

George Nearly came apart at the seams.

Linda He didn't look too bad.

George He's hiding it well.

Bernard comes in from the patio. He is holding a piece of greenery plus root

Bernard Ah! Daughter-in-law, can I have your opinion. Is this a weed or one of your herbs?

Linda moves away DL *to collect her bag by the TV. Bernard takes in the situation*

Oh. Intruding, eh?

Linda Not really. We were discussing Leonard and—us.

Bernard Oh. Well, Leonard's young. Youth is very resilient.

George I suppose I had a long chat with you last night as well, did I?

Bernard No, I got all my information from that funny speech you made from the top of the piano.

George groans and buries his head

Linda It needn't affect you, you know, Bernard. (*She goes above the settee to* UC)

George Oh, no! Don't let my moving out affect or inconvenience anybody else.

Linda I mean, this is your home too, Dad.

Bernard Yes. Well. Talk about it. Work to do. (*He moves to the windows*)

Linda I think he's pretty shattered.

George *He's* shattered!

Bernard (*stopping*) By the way—herb or weed?

Roger enters from the patio and surveys the "weed"

Roger *Funiculum vulgare.*

Bernard Oh, is it? I'd better bung it back then.

Bernard exits through the windows

Roger Hello you two.

Linda Hello Roger.

Roger crosses Linda to survey George

Roger Just thought I'd drop in—see how George is feeling.

George Dreadful.

Linda Where's Betty?

Roger Doing some housework. Re-polishing the top of the piano.

George Oh, Gawd!

Roger (*to Linda*) She says if you feel like popping over for a natter before lunch you'd be very welcome.

Linda I think I might like that.

Roger Don't worry, I'll cheer George up. I'll tell him some of my funny stories.

Linda Yes. Tell him the one about the honeymoon and the flamenco dancer.

Linda exits into the kitchen with the shopping bag, leaving the other shopping bag by the table DR

Roger (*moving behind the settee*) I don't know that one. I do know a limerick about a nun, actually:

> "There was an old monk of Siberia,
> Whose morals were slightly inferior,
> He done to a nun what none should have done,
> And now she's a Mother Superior".

Roger laughs. George doesn't. Roger moves DL *and sits on the* L *end of the settee*

Well, how are you feeling, mate?

George Bloody awful! The last twenty-four hours have been the worst in my life.

Roger You were lucky you didn't break your neck falling down our stairs.

George I know. I repeated the feat here.

Roger You didn't?!

George Yes. Do you know Roger, I can't remember a thing about last night. Did I really get up on that piano?

Roger Yes. You were pretty pissed.

George Then how did I get up on the piano?

Roger I gave you a boost. I was pretty pissed too.

George Honestly, Roger, I'm sorry.

Roger (*dismissing it*) Oh, I don't care about the piano. I never liked it. Betty's mother gave it to us. I was a little put out about the fish in my aquarium though.

George (*apprehensively*) Aquarium?

Roger Don't you remember that either?

George No.

Roger You poured a double gin into it.

George No! Why should I do a thing like that, I love animals.

Roger We had a little bet. You bet me a fiver that with a couple of drinks inside him the guppy could beat the living daylights out of the Siamese fighting fish.

George shakes his head in disbelief. Roger hands him a £5 note

Here. You won.

George (*waving it away*) No, keep it.

Roger It's yours.

George I couldn't. Give it to the RSPCA.

Roger OK. Don't worry about the fish though. They've never looked so good. I might even add a little gin to the water each day. (*Happily*) Anyway, all your friends were delighted to hear about your vasectomy— and the flamenco dancer.

George What a bloody mess!

Roger (*rising*) Is there a drink going in this place?

George (*waving vaguely*) You know where it is.

Roger (*gently*) Hey, I can't tell you how sorry I feel about you and Linda.

George Thanks, Roger.

Roger When are you moving out? (*He moves to pour himself a drink*)

George (*bemused*) This afternoon, I think. I'll book into the *Swan Hotel* in Epsom.

Roger Very nice.

George And then I'll get a flat I suppose.

Roger Well, whatever happens—I want you to know I'm around any time you need.

George (*touched*) I appreciate that, Roger.

Roger returns to sit on the L end of the settee with his drink

Roger And be prepared, George, because you're going to have a tremendous emotional reaction——

George (*agreeing*) I am.

Roger —and you're going to be faced with a hell of a lot of added expense.

George (*surprised*) Am I?

Roger Bound to be. It's going to be legal and it's going to be expensive.

George Is it? (*Bewildered*) I just can't believe all this is happening.

Roger And I'd like to help out financially.

George The whole thing is so——(*He stops, realizing what Roger has said. Slightly embarrassed*) That's very kind of you Roger, but I'll be able to manage, honestly.

Roger No, I insist. At least in the beginning. You're going to have to find this flat and that's double expenses for a start. I'd like to come in for, say, twenty pounds a week.

George No, Roger.

Roger I *want* to. As I say, it's going to be expensive.

George Look, I don't care. I just want to think of some way of persuading Linda to change her mind.

Roger I'll make it thirty pounds a week.

George Roger—I'm sure it will be expensive, but how can I take money from you for a flat when I'm the one that's going to be using it?

Roger (*trying to be off-hand*) Well, if it will make you feel any better—I'll use it too.

George How do you mean?
Roger On occasions.
George On occasions?
Roger Every Monday and Wednesday.
George (*realizing*) Oh no!
Roger George! Please! Sid Taylor's boat goes into dry dock next week and I've got nowhere to take Raquel.
George Roger, it's a question of morality.
Roger OK, OK. I understand how you feel, and I respect you for that.
George Good.
Roger I'll make it fifty quid a week.
George No!

Linda, in an emotional state, hurries in through the french windows

Roger quickly rises and nonchalantly moves above the settee to meet Linda at C

Linda Roger!
Roger Oh, hi Linda. You weren't long.
Linda No. Betty wants you back right away.
Roger She's all right, isn't she?
Linda Oh yes. It's just that Judy's suddenly arrived.
Roger Judy? Sid's Judy?
Linda Judy Taylor, yes.
Roger Why isn't she on the boat with Sid?
Linda I couldn't quite follow it all. Judy was pretty hysterical. I don't know where Sid is. It appears they're selling the boat.
Roger Selling it? I thought Sid was putting it into dry dock.
Linda No, Judy's making him sell it.
Roger Why, for heaven's sake?
Linda From what I can gather they're going to need the money for Sid to see a psychiatrist.
Roger Psychiatrist?! What's the matter with him?
Linda He's become a transvestite.
Roger (*in disbelief*) A transvestite?
George That's a gentleman that dresses up in lady's——
Roger (*shouting*) I know what a transvestite is! (*To Linda*) Where on earth did anybody get the idea that Sid Taylor was one of those?
Linda Apparently Sid admitted it.
Roger (*amazed*) What?
George No, I can't believe it of Sid, he smokes a pipe.

Roger and Linda turn and glare at George

Roger (*to Linda*) Not Sid!
Linda Yes. Judy told us everything. She found a bra and a pair of frilly pants on the boat and Sid confessed they were his.

There is a pause as George and Roger look at each other

Linda picks up the bag of groceries and exits into the kitchen

George laughs and wags a finger at the confused Roger

George "Oh, what a tangled web we weave when first we practise——"

Roger Oh, shut up! (*He hurries to the windows but quickly returns to George*)
I'll make it seventy-five pounds a week!

George No!

Betty hurries in from the french windows in a state

Betty Roger, you'd better come back quickly! Sorry about this, George.

Roger What's happened now?

Betty Has Linda told you about Judy turning up?

Roger Yes.

Betty And about Sid's transvestite business?

Roger Yes!

Betty Well *Sid's* arrived now.

Roger At our place?

Betty Yes.

George Wearing his winter dress, is he?

Betty It's not funny, George.

Roger No, it's not funny, George.

George You're right, it's not funny. It's bloody hysterical.

Roger I'd better get over there in case they come to blows.

Roger rushes out

George (*shouting after him*) Smack Sid's wrist if he turns spiteful.

Betty What a morning.

George What a night.

Betty I'm so sorry, George—about you and Linda.

George I'm sorry too—about your piano and your Siamese fighting fish.

Betty Well, as my mother used to say—nothing matters half as much as you
think it does.

George Bit of a philosopher was she, your mother?

Betty Yes. She had a motto for most occasions.

George Didn't she have anything better than "Nothing matters half as
much as you think it does"?

Betty "Every cloud has a silver lining"?

George (*miserably*) Terrific!

Betty Oh, come on George. Look on the bright side.

George You take after your mother, don't you?

Betty It may even be all right if you give her time.

George God, it's no different from most marriages, is it?

Betty No. (*Brightly*) Well, soon be Christmas!

George Betty!

Betty Well, I'd better get back to Judy and Sid. (*She goes up to the windows*)

George Yes. You do that.

Betty (*stopping*) And George!

George Yes?

Betty Keep your pecker up!

Betty exits through the french windows

George reacts, then rises and sadly moves DL *to look at his wedding photo*

Linda comes out of the kitchen and moves towards the stairs

George Linda . . .

She stops, her back to George

This is madness. Let's give it a couple of weeks.

Linda shakes her head. George moves up to her

Hey! Maybe I could grab some time off. We'd go away. Brighton, Torquay—Torremolinos.

Linda glares at him

Betty rushes in from the french windows

Betty George! Quick!
George (*flatly*) Is it Judy or Sid?
Betty It's your father.
George (*hesitating*) Dad?
Betty He was just lying there on the lawn.

George and Linda look at each other

Linda George.

Roger wheels in a prostrate Bernard in the wheelbarrow

Roger Sorry, George, this is all that was handy.
Linda I'll phone the doctor. (*She rushes to the phone*)
George Christ. He's not dead, is he?
Bernard (*dazed; as he sits up*) I trod on the bloody garden rake.

Everybody reacts

CURTAIN

ACT II

The Harpers' living-room. Early evening on Christmas Eve

The gaudy curtains have been replaced by something more feminine and the lampshades and cushions are softer. There is a Christmas tree plus lights and decorations with presents around it in front of the french windows. Christmas cards and decorations are around the room. There is a piece of sculpture, about two feet high and obviously by a novice, on the drinks cabinet. The wedding photo has been replaced by a beginner's oil painting

The curtains are open and the patio lights are on. Snow can be seen falling. The main lights are off, but the Christmas tree lights are on. A pair of step ladders is upstage. Leonard's shoes are by the fireplace. Leonard is adjusting the Christmas tree lights. An upbeat rock number is playing on the record player

After a moment, Betty comes in from the kitchen. She is wearing an anorak and carrying some wrapped Christmas presents. She is covered with snow

Betty (*shouting above the music*) Anyone home?
Leonard Oh, hi, Betty.
Betty Hello, Leonard. Snow's really coming down now.
Leonard Hang on a sec. (*He turns the record off and switches on the main lights*) Sorry about that.
Betty Snow's getting quite thick.
Leonard Yeah, brill. (*He takes the record off the turntable and puts it away*)
Betty Your mum not around?
Leonard No, she's at one of her classes. Aerobics, I think.
Betty That was yesterday.
Leonard Oh. Maybe it's sculpting again today. I don't know. I can't keep track.
Betty Yes, it makes me exhausted just thinking about her. I've brought our pressies over.
Leonard Brill. Shove 'em under the tree, will you?
Betty OK. Not to be opened until tomorrow.
Leonard I know!

During the ensuing dialogue Leonard climbs the ladder and fixes a hanging Christmas decoration

Betty Has your dad arrived yet?
Leonard Not yet, no.

Betty I must say, it hasn't been the same without George around. I didn't think your mum would last four weeks.

Leonard Neither did I.

Betty Poor old George. It must be agony having to stay away.

Leonard Yes. He rings up though.

Betty That's nice.

Leonard Yes. Never less than three times a day.

Bernard comes downstairs wearing a complete Father Christmas outfit but minus beard. The outfit is rather tatty

Bernard Anyone seen my beard?

Leonard I've told you, Grandad, it's in that box in the attic.

Bernard Looked there.

Leonard It's in the box marked "OXO". (*He moves his ladder to the fireplace to hang up decorations*)

Bernard Oh. OXO.

Betty Hi, sexy Santa!

Bernard Mrs D! Come on, give us a Christmas Eve kiss.

Betty gives him a kiss on his cheek

Betty I'm glad to see you're giving us your Father Christmas again this year.

Bernard (*moving* DC) Oh yes. Got to keep up the traditions, haven't we, Leonard?

Leonard You bet.

Betty (*joining Bernard* DC) Quite right.

Bernard (*referring to his suit*) I'm afraid this is going home, though. My wife made it, you know. Clever lady my wife.

Betty She must have been. She married you, didn't she?

Bernard Thirty-nine years we had. Walked down the aisle in an air-raid. Yes. And our marriage was one long air-raid for thirty-nine years.

Betty (*laughing*) I can't believe that.

Bernard Yes, it was! I tell you—compared to my wife, Hitler was a pussy cat.

Leonard Grandad, hold that for us will you?

Leonard hands Bernard the end of a hanging decoration

Bernard Well, we RAF johnnies must have been dashed difficult to live with, especially after the war. Maybe *that's* George's trouble. I hardly saw him really until he was six or seven. Mummy's boy. When I was demobbed he and I spent the first six months arguing over which one of us was going to sleep with Mummy. Unfortunately, I won.

Betty chuckles

Leonard Thanks, Grandad. (*He takes back the decoration*)

Betty (*to Bernard*) Go and find your beard!

Bernard I'll have a look. (*To Betty*) Are we Christmas lunching with you tomorrow?

Betty No, dinner. But we're coming over here in the morning for coffee and pressies.

Bernard Whacko! White Christmas, too. Exciting, isn't it? Snowballs, Leonard.

Leonard Yeah, brill!

Bernard Come on. Give us another Christmas Eve kiss.

Betty You're not getting another kiss without mistletoe.

Bernard produces a sprig of mistletoe. Betty laughs and gives him another kiss

Bernard Did you say "OXO" or "Bovril"?

Leonard I'll come with you.

Bernard (*saluting*) Good thinking. Always reconnoitre in pairs. Leonard, did I ever tell you about the Christmas that Jumbo Phillpots, Jock McIntosh and I spent in nineteen forty-one?

As they start up the stairs, the front doorbell goes

Betty I'll get it, I'm just off.

Bernard and Leonard exit

Betty opens the door

George is standing there in his overcoat and cap, covered in snow. He carries several wrapped presents

George!

George (*awkwardly*) Oh. Hello, Betty.

Betty Linda's not back yet.

George I'm a bit early actually.

Betty Happy Christmas. (*She kisses him on the cheek*)

George Yes. Happy Christmas.

Betty I was just dropping off the presents.

George Oh, nice. Yes. Me, too. It's snowing.

Betty (*laughing*) No, I thought it was dandruff.

George (*seriously*) No. It's snow.

Betty All OK with you?

George Oh. Everything's fantastic.

Betty That's the attitude. "It's easy enough to be pleasant when life goes along with a song, but the man worthwhile is the one who can smile, when everything goes dead wrong".

George gives her a blank stare and walks to the tree with his presents

Don't forget, as usual, you and Linda are coming over for Christmas punch later.

George Er—no. *I* won't, but I'm sure Linda will.

Betty Aren't you staying the night?

George Er—no.

Betty Hell, I was banking on that putting everything right.

George, to avoid the issue, walks in front of her to the fireplace and surveys the cards

George Roger said he'd be over at seven o'clock.
Betty He'll be here.
George It's very good of him to help out, actually. The last thing I want is for Linda and me to fall out over the maintenance. And, as Roger said, somehow a solicitor makes it all seem so final.
Betty You should be discussing a reconciliation, not maintenance.
George Yes, well, anyway, Roger's a real whizz-kid at figures, isn't he?
Betty You can say that again. He hasn't paid any income tax since nineteen seventy-three.
George (*genuinely surprised*) Hasn't he?

Leonard hurries downstairs carrying a Christmas decoration

Leonard Oh, hi, Dad.
George Hi, son. Great to see you.

George goes to hug Leonard but Leonard, unthinking, goes right past him to arrange the decoration

Leonard What do you think of the decorations this year?
George (*bravely*) Super.
Leonard Me and Grandad did the lot.
George Really super.
Leonard I reckon they're the best we've ever had.
George Yes, very sensitive.
Betty I'll get back to my mince pies, George. And you'll be in good hands with Roger.
George Yes! I mean if he hasn't paid any income tax since nineteen seventy-three—how's he managed that, by the way?
Betty Well, he just sends the tax returns back with "Gone away and died" written on them.

Betty exits through the kitchen

George takes in the room

George I say—it's different.
Leonard Yes. Superbrill.
George I mean, the room's different.
Leonard Oh, yes. Mum went berserk. New lampshades. Cushion covers. New carpets. New curtains. (*He pulls the curtains closed*)
George New curtains, yes. Very nice. What on earth is this? (*He points to the oil painting* DL)
Leonard Mum's first painting.
George What happened to our wedding photo?
Leonard Well, we thought that made the place look a bit more cheerful. (*He moves upstage and puts the ladders in the cloakroom*)
George She's all right, is she, your mother?

Leonard Yeah, ultrabrill. We haven't seen much of each other. I only broke up last Friday and Mum's been out all the time.

George Out?

Leonard Going to all her classes. So far she's taken up aerobics, sculpting, fencing, French and painting.

George moves to below the settee

George Nice to see she's keeping herself occupied. (*Referring to the sculpture*) And this is an example of her sculpting, is it? (*He moves to the drinks cabinet*)

Leonard Yeah. Michaelangelo is issuing a writ. (*He puts on a thick skiing jacket*)

George Fancy a Coke or beer?

Leonard No, thanks.

George I think I'll have one.

Leonard joins George

Leonard You've had one already, haven't you, Dad?

George How do you mean?

Leonard (*laughing*) I can tell.

George Dutch Courage, as a matter of fact.

Leonard What for?

George Tonight. We're working out the settlement. Alimony, you know. Maintenance for you and your mother.

Leonard Well, will you bear in mind that Mum's increased my pocket money by one pound fifty.

George nods

Right, I'm off then.

George Where are you going?

Leonard Pictures. I'm taking Geraldine.

George Geraldine?

Leonard Geraldine Thomsett. She's seventeen and ten months. Dead sexy. Drives her own car.

George Leonard—I hope you're careful.

Leonard She doesn't drive fast.

George I'm not talking about driving. I'm talking about parking.

Leonard Parking?

George I know what you children get up to. I was young once.

Leonard Why do we want to bother with parking? Geraldine's got a flat.

George reacts. Leonard moves away to get his shoes

George Well son—I don't want to know what you get up to——

Leonard (*grinning*) That's good. I don't want to tell you.

George But, remember, you're a responsible person. And—er—well, as I said—you be careful.

Leonard You don't have to worry, Dad.

George Good.

Leonard Geraldine's on the Pill. (*He gets his shoes and sits on the L arm of the settee putting them on*)
George (*nonplussed*) Oh. Well—er—I suppose if she's nearly eighteen.
Leonard She's been on it for two years now.

George moves behind the settee and comes DL on Leonard's L

George Oh. Well—er—I can't say I approve. In fact, I don't but—er—I still think it might be safer—er—wiser for you to—er—you know—wear something.
Leonard A funny hat?
George *Wear* something.
Leonard Oh, come off it, Dad.
George You go to that chemist by the station and buy some.
Leonard I can't do that. They know me there.
George It's nothing to be embarrassed about.
Leonard Like hell it isn't. The chemist is Geraldine's father. (*He rises and moves in front of the settee and up to the front door*)
George Oh.
Leonard I've got to go. See you, Dad.

George moves up to Leonard's L

George Tell Geraldine to drive carefully on these roads.
Leonard OK.
George And, Leonard ...
Leonard Yes?
George Treat her gently. I mean, it's important. Whether it lasts a few weeks or seventeen years—it's important.
Leonard OK.

They shake hands as the doorbell rings

George And you should be going to Church on Christmas Eve, not the cinema.
Leonard You're probably right, Dad. Are you and Mum going to Church?
George Good-night Leonard.

Leonard opens the door

    Roger enters. He is wearing a snow-covered overcoat and carrying a briefcase

Roger Hello there, Leonard.
Leonard See you, Rog!

    Leonard gives Roger a playful punch and exits

Roger looks after him nods, and closes the door

Roger He's growing up.
George You can say that again. Whisky?

George moves to the drinks cabinet as Roger removes his coat and hangs it over the balustrade

Roger Thanks.

George It's a real eye-opener.

Roger (*referring to the drink*) Not too much water. (*He moves* DL *and sits on the* L *end of the settee*)

George There's Leonard, still only sixteen with a seventeen-year-old nymphomaniac who's on the Pill and got her own flat.

Roger It's disgraceful—lucky sod! Betty says you're not coming over for Christmas punch tonight.

George comes behind the settee and gives Roger his drink

George No. I need to get back to the flat.

Roger Cheers—er . . .

George Linda's not home yet. (*He takes a swig of his drink*)

Roger Ah. You'd better not have too much tonight, George, or you'll be up on the piano telling funny stories.

George breaks away C

George (*expansively*) I'm fine. It's good of you to come over, Roger.

Roger Pleasure, George, pleasure. (*He grins*) And I'm cheaper than a solicitor.

George It's not that but solicitors make it seem like a company going into liquidation.

Roger We'll sort it out amicably. Although some friends of mine from up North are just going through a very tough divorce. Lots of bitterness there, I can tell you.

George Dear oh dear. (*He sits on the* R *end of the settee*)

Roger They just can't agree on the children.

George That's terrible.

Roger Yes. Neither one wants them. So how do you like being a bachelor?

George I don't like it. I don't like living alone. I could weep.

Roger So don't be alone. There's a lot of nice looking girls in East Grinstead.

George (*tersely*) I'm not interested in girls!

Roger What about women?

George It's been over seventeen years. I wouldn't know what to say to a woman. I'm used to talking to my wife.

Roger Seriously, old son, you've got to start doing something about your sex life. I mean to say, four weeks—don't you get headaches?

George (*blankly*) Headaches?

Roger If you haven't had your oats for over four weeks—you must get headaches.

George No.

Roger I had sex with Betty this morning and I've got a headache just hearing about you.

George (*after a pause*) Do you do that often?

Roger What?
George Make love in the morning.
Roger Naturally.
George Do you really?
Roger Well, not on the mornings I play golf. Why?
George No reason. It's just that there were—er—times when Linda and I were alone in the afternoon and—er—she wanted to make love.
Roger (*interested*) Did she?
George Yes. On the rug in front of the fire.
Roger I say.
George In the winter, that would be, of course.
Roger Of course. Mind you, you'd have to be careful, wouldn't you? Might burn your bum. (*He chortles*)
George We never did it though.
Roger Why not?
George I don't know. It was me. To me, sex has always been something I do during the night.
Roger You'd be a riot in Greenland.

Roger sips his drink as George tries to assimilate this last remark. Finally George gives up and looks at his watch

Linda's late.
George Yes.
Roger As long as we're through by eight. I've got to slip along to the hospital.
George Hospital?
Roger Raquel is in Woking General Hospital.
George Oh dear.
Roger Slipped a disc a couple of weeks ago. Before Sid sold the boat.
George Oh, that all happened, did it?
Roger Yes. We'd had the most marvellous night—and morning—then she went and slipped coming down the gangplank.
George Is she all right?
Roger Yes, but she's in traction.
George Traction? You mean——?
Roger Yes. (*He sticks his leg in the air*)
George Poor girl.
Roger I hope the hospital let me in tonight.
George Why shouldn't they?
Roger The last time I was there the nurse walked in and caught me in bed with Raquel.
George (*staring at him*) Roger, you didn't? Not while she was in——(*He sticks his leg in the air*)
Roger (*quickly pointing at George's leg*) That's what set me off.
George (*hastily crossing his legs*) Roger! You're an animal.
Roger (*laughing*) You can say that again! You need to be a kangaroo to end up in the position we were in.

George You're hopeless! Didn't you realize the nurse might walk in and catch you.

Roger She wouldn't have done if the old lady in the next bed hadn't come out of her coma at that moment and screamed.

George looks staggered then tries not to laugh. George rises and goes to top up his glass

George How are Sid and Judy by the way? I mean, Sid didn't give you away did he?

Roger No.

George Well, what happened about that transvestite business?

Roger That's fine. Judy's totally accepted it.

George (*amazed*) Has she? (*He moves to* C *with his drink*)

Roger It's given their marriage a whole new lease of life. Not only does Sid now dress up in Judy's clothes, but Judy's taken to going to bed wearing Sid's sailing jacket and his rubber boots.

They both laugh

Bernard enters from the stairs

Bernard Leonard! Leonard! Has Leonard gone?

George Hello, Dad!

Bernard I still can't find it.

George What?

Bernard My Father Christmas beard.

George How are you?

Bernard You haven't seen it knocking around, have you?

George I've been away four weeks.

Bernard Is it as long as that? Yes, you look thinner. Looks thinner, doesn't he, Roger?

Roger Yes. Missing his oats.

George Roger, please! I don't know where Linda can have got to.

Bernard Linda. Ah! Yes, she phoned. Left a message for you.

George Phoned?

Bernard Yes. Middle of the afternoon. I meant to write it down.

George What was it?

Bernard What was what?

George The message!

Bernard Er—I knew I should have written it down. She's going to be late.

George Is that all?

Bernard She was in a bit of a hurry. Phoning from the *Savoy Hotel*.

George and Roger exchange a glance

Roger *Savoy Hotel?*

George In the middle of the afternoon? (*Laughing*) You've got it all wrong, Dad.

Bernard No, no, no.

George What would Linda be doing in the *Savoy Hotel?*

Bernard (*smiling*) In my young days there'd only be one reason for spending the afternoon in the *Savoy Hotel*, eh Roger?
Roger Absolutely right, Bernard.

Bernard and Roger chuckle as George looks blank

George (*finally*) What's that?

Bernard and Roger react

Bernard George, if your brains were made of doughnuts, you wouldn't have enough for the hole in the middle.

Bernard exits upstairs

George slowly realizes the implication

George (*slowly*) Savoy Hotel?
Roger Now don't jump to conclusions.
George (*in disbelief*) Roger—you don't think——
Roger (*laughing*) No. Not Linda.
George Wait a minute! All this nonsense about aerobics and French. She's been with some fellow.
Roger George, she's not the kind——
George (*pressing on*) While she's carrying on left, right and centre, I'm sitting in my flat every night with these terrible headaches!

Linda enters, looking fantastic. She carries a carrier bag, and smiles radiantly at them

Roger and George exchange a look

Where have you been?
Linda (*sweetly, with a French accent*) Bon Noël, Roger. Bon Noël, mon petit George.

George and Roger look at each other

George (*to Linda*) Never mind (*With an overdone French accent*) "Bon Noël, Roger. Bon Noël, mon petit George." (*Still with an accent*) Where 'ave you been? (*Correcting himself*) I mean—where have you been?
Roger Excuse me old son——
George Shut up!
Linda Is George upset about the settlement or something?
George (*derisively*) Settlement!
Roger I'll make some coffee for him.
George I don't want any coffee.
Roger We've had a little drink. I think George may have had a couple before.
George Never mind about what *I've* had.
Roger (*quickly*) I'll make some coffee.
Linda Thanks, I'd love one.

Roger exits to the kitchen

George Come on—where have you been?
Linda If you must know I've been buying some Christmas presents for Leonard.
George Christmas presents for Leonard?! You did that weeks ago.
Linda After my shopping I popped into the *Savoy* for tea.
George Tea!! Christmas presents for Leonard! You've been with a man, haven't you?
Linda A man?
George A proper man! Open that bag! You've got your sexy nightie in there! And your toothbrush!
Linda (*after a pause*) Very well, George. You're right. I've been seeing someone ever since you left. We spend most afternoons in a suite at the *Savoy*. And today. (*She opens the carrier bag*) I was so good in bed that he gave me a Christmas annual and a pair of football boots.

She takes out football boots and an annual and gives them to George. George hesitates. They look at each other. Linda laughs, George hesitates and then he, too, laughs

George (*finally*) I'm sorry.
Linda That's all right.
George It's not like me—behaving like a jealous nutcase.
Linda (*smiling*) You don't have to apologize to me for being jealous. I'm flattered.
George Are you?
Linda I think it's the first time I've ever seen you jealous. (*She takes her coat off and hangs it in the cloakroom*)
George Jealousy is one of the things that ruins marriages. Do you mind if I smoke?
Linda Go ahead. I haven't been able to stop you in seventeen years.

George taps his pipe out in the bowl of the statue

(*Aghast*) What are you doing?
George I'm just——(*He taps his pipe again*)
Linda That's not an ashtray.
George Oh, isn't it?
Linda (*levelly*) It's a Roman girl carrying a bowl.
George I thought it was "Britannia having a baby".

George chortles merrily. There is a pause and then Linda bursts into tears. George is amazed

What's the matter? Linda, dear—what did I say?

Linda can only howl, point at the statue and mumble, incoherently

Roger comes in breezily from the kitchen with coffee

Roger Coffee up. (*He quickly takes in the situation*) I'll make some sandwiches as well.

Roger exits into the kitchen

George Linda, I'm sorry. I wouldn't upset you for the world. I didn't know you took your sculpting rubbish seriously. (*He picks the statue up*)

Linda howls again

I think you show a lot of promise as a sculptress. (*He refers to the bowl*) This is very nice.

Linda sniffs

And I like the way you've changed the room. What have you done with my old curtains by the way?

Linda looks at him

Linda (*bursting into tears*) I burnt them! (*She sits on the R end of the settee*)

George replaces the statue

Bernard enters down the stairs, still wearing the outfit, plus beard. He comes to George's L

Bernard I found it. Chocks away! Scramble! George! (*He pulls the beard down*) It's me! Good to see you son. You look thinner. Looks thinner, doesn't he, Linda?
Linda (*blinking through tears*) Yes.
Bernard Ah. Having a family discussion, eh?
George Yes, we are, Dad.
Bernard Right. Where's young Leonard?
George He's gone out.
Bernard Pity. We were going to play snowballs. (*Remembering*) Where's Gertie?

Linda rises and pushes Bernard to the kitchen

Linda In the kitchen, I expect, Dad. Look, why don't you make a start on your turkey stuffing?
Bernard Right. Hurricane's Special Stuffing, eh? Oh, and I've got something for Gertie. Found it in the attic. I made it when she was a puppy. Christmas nineteen eighty. (*He takes out of his pocket a small Father Christmas hat. Calling*) Gertie!

Bernard exits into the kitchen

Linda sits in the armchair DR

George Are you all right now?
Linda I think so. I've been in a bit of a state actually since you left.
George Have you?
Linda Sort of . . . frightened.
George You've got a good lock on the door.
Linda I don't mean that. Frightened of being just me by myself.
George That's why we're separated, isn't it? So that you can be you by yourself.
Linda Yes.

George moves down to the table by the armchair

George Linda, the more I listen to you, the more I realize how ridiculous
this whole separation is. I mean, I don't want to be me by myself any more
than you want to be you by yourself.
Linda It's no good George. We'll just make the same mistakes all over
again.
George No we won't. We'll make different ones.

*Roger tentatively puts his head in. He is carrying a tray on which are coffee
and sandwiches. He is also wearing the small Father Christmas hat*

Roger Coffee and sandwiches?

*George breaks upstage. Roger moves behind Linda and puts the tray on the
table*

Linda Thanks, Roger.
Roger Do you like the hat?
Linda (*smiling*) Suits you.
Roger Yes. Bernard gave it to me. He said he knew it was for somebody but
couldn't remember who. Well, let's get down to business. (*He gets his
briefcase*)
George Roger, we've been thinking——
Linda No, we haven't!
George Why don't we postpone this for a week.
Linda No!

Roger looks at George

George All right.

George moves to top up his glass as Roger sets a chair from upstage

Linda Coffee, George?
George (*brightly*) No, I'll stick to alcohol for the moment, thank you. How
about you, Roger?

Roger moves down and sits L of the table

Roger Small one. I'm on duty now. You ought to take it easy too, George.
George No, no. I'm capably totable.

Linda and Roger exchange a glance

Linda Nice looking sandwiches, Roger.
Roger Bernard made them. Cold ham and Hurricane's Special Stuffing.
Now, George, I suggest the way we handle this is to start by making out
some sort of expense sheet. See roughly how much Linda needs to live on.
George (*fairly*) Fine, fine.
Roger Linda, you said you were going to work out roughly what your
expenses are.

Linda rises and steps up to the drinks cabinet

Linda I've done as best I can. (*She gets two folders from the shelves, hands Roger a folder and keeps the other one for herself*)
Roger This is very well set out.
Linda I got a bit of help actually.
Roger Jolly good.
Linda From one of the women I met on my Awareness Course. Sandwich, Roger?

George moves down between them, above the table

George On your what?
Linda My Awareness Course. It's a fascinating course run by the Local Council. Sandwich, George?
George I wasn't aware that you'd joined an Awareness Course.
Roger Well, you would be if you were on an Awareness Course!

Roger guffaws at his own joke. George doesn't think it's funny and glares at him. Linda suddenly sees the joke and laughs. George glares at her

Linda Don't you get it, George? If you were on my Awareness Course you'd see me and know I was there. At the same time if you were taking the Awareness Course you'd be more aware. It's a double joke.
George Oh, I see! A double joke——
Linda ⎱ (*together*)⎰ Yes!
Roger ⎰   ⎱
George Yes, it's twice as unfunny as I thought it was.

Linda doesn't find that amusing. George does and ambles away to the fireplace

Roger (*quickly*) Let's get down to business.
Linda It's all right, Roger. I'm not offended. There was a time when if George said something like that it would have crushed me. But not any more. I can handle it now.
Roger Jolly good. Right——!
George You never mentioned your Awareness Course, that's all I said.
Linda I didn't think you'd be interested.
George Well, of course I'm interested in what you're doing with yourself.
Linda I wasn't aware of it.
George It doesn't sound as though that Awareness Course is doing you much good.

George bursts into laughter. Linda doesn't. Roger steps in quickly

Roger That isn't funny, old son.
George Why not? It was when you said it.
Linda That's all right, Roger. I can handle that, too.

George moves above the settee towards them

George Handle what, too?
Linda Your resentment over the fact that I'm growing, improving myself, that I'm accomplishing things without you.
George I don't resent it. (*He moves to Roger*) Did I say I resented anything?

Roger Er—no. (*To Linda*) I don't think—er——

George (*to Linda*) Have I said I resented anything?

Linda (*to Roger*) George has been trying to punish himself for years and I'm not going to help him any more. They made me realize that at my Awareness Course.

Roger (*to George*) There we are. They did some good. Right——!

George (*to Linda*) What do you mean—I've been trying to punish myself?

Linda It's a game you and I played for seventeen years and I'm not playing it any more. Because now I know who you are.

George takes in this profound remark

George Well, you've certainly made a lot of progress. (*To Roger*) She broke up our marriage to find out who *she* was and so far all she's found out is who *I* am.

There is a pause

Who am I?

Linda You'll find it hard to believe at first . . .

George looks at Roger and then back to Linda

George Who am I?

Linda My mother.

George considers this

George I'm your mother?

Linda That's right. I married my mother. And do you know who you married?

George I'm beginning to wonder.

Linda I'll tell you.

George Thank you.

Linda You married your father.

George No, he's not my type.

Linda (*to Roger*) You see, you can't discuss anything with him.

Roger Not too easy to take in at first, old girl.

George Absolutely!

Roger Right——!

Linda It's really quite simple once you understand transference. I have transferred all the feelings for my mother to George and George has transferred all the feelings for his father to me.

Roger I see. You married your mother and he married his father.

Linda That's it.

George Then why are we separating? We're brother and sister. (*He goes to pour himself another drink*)

Roger Right, let's get back to business.

George Yes, sock it to me, sister! (*He is now pleasantly sloshed*)

Roger What's on your list, Linda?

Linda I'll start at the beginning.

George What a very good idea!

Linda Household expenses and food.
George Food. Good. Got to eat. (*He sits on the* R *arm of the settee*)
Linda For Leonard and myself.
George Good. Growing boy. And Dad.
Linda Dad, too, yes.
Roger Food, three persons.
George And Gertie.

Roger glares at George

Roger Three persons, plus *dog*.
Linda Clothing.
George Clothing.
Roger Three persons, clothing.
George Plus one dog lead.

Roger glares

   Sorry!
Linda Medical expenses. Pills, potions, tablets, etc.
George Medical expenses. Got to keep fit.
Roger Medical expenses——
George Plus vet.
Roger (*angrily*) Plus vet.
George And VAT.
Roger (*more angrily*) And VAT.
Linda "Entertainment" all right?
Roger OK George?
George You bet, entertainment, three persons.
Roger Entertainment.
George No entertainment for Gertie, bad dog, Gertie!

George chuckles as Roger glares at him

Linda Leonard's school fees.
George School fees, one juvenile person.
Roger School fees!

Linda is now beginning to get cross

Linda Oil, gas, electricity, rates.
George Oil, gas, electricity, rates!
Roger Oil, gas, electricity, rates.
Linda Car maintenance and running expenses!!
George Car maintenance and running expenses.
Roger Car maintenance and running expenses.
Linda House maintenance and repairs!!
George House maintenance and repairs, and eyes down for a full house!
   (*He laughs and collapses on to the settee*)
Roger George, please! House maintenance and repairs.
Linda Hairdressing.
Roger (*to George*) Hairdressing?

George Yes. Not Dad. Just Linda, Leonard and Gertie.
Roger Hairdressing.
George Two persons, one dog.
Linda Upkeep of garden.
George Yep!
Roger Upkeep of garden.
Linda Mortgage payments and insurances.
George Yep.
Roger Mortage payments and insurances.
Linda Travel expenses when not using car.
George Yep, train, bus, tube, OK.
Roger Travel expenses, three persons——
George No! One person, one student, one OAP.
Linda That's pretty much it.
George Great! No problems.
Roger That comes to one hundred and eight-five pounds.
George One hundred and eighty-five pounds a month. Cheap at the price.
Linda One hundred and eighty-five pounds a *week*, dear.

George takes this in

George A *week*?
Linda Yes, dear.
George One hundred and eight-five pounds a *week*!?
Linda Yes.
George We didn't spend that when we were *married*!
Roger Excuse me George——
George Shut up! (*To Linda*) I have to live too, you know.
Linda I'm perfectly aware of that, George.
George Oh, are you? Then how come all we're talking about is what *you* need.
Roger Because *you're* the *breadwinner*.
George Let her eat cake!
Roger Steady on, George. There's no need to get upset.
George *I'm* not upset. I just don't like being taken for a mug, that's all.
Linda Who's taking you for a mug?
George You and Perry Mason here. (*He goes to refill his whisky glass*)
Roger Now, let's not argue. We'll start from the beginning to see if we can cut down a little.
George (*adamant*) You mean cut down a lot. What have you got for food?
Roger Forty-five pounds a week.
George Make it fifteen.
Linda How can we eat on that? You said yourself Leonard's a growing boy.
George Tell him to stop growing, he's tall enough.
Roger Be reasonable, George.
George When I want your advice, I'll ask for it.
Roger You *did* ask for it. That's what I'm doing here. And fifteen pounds a week for food does not seem fair to me.

George thrusts his face close to Roger

George Or course it doesn't seem fair to you! You and Linda are in this together.
Linda That's silly.
George (*turning to her*) You keep out of this. (*Nose to nose with Roger again*) You and Linda and Betty are all in cahoots, aren't you?
Linda George, you're sloshed.
George Will you keep quiet, please. (*Nose to nose with Roger again*) You can take your expense sheet and go back to your barmaid. (*He snatches the expense sheet from Roger*)
Roger (*warningly*) George!
Linda (*puzzled*) What does a barmaid have to do with it?
George Plenty. (*He points to Roger*) He's trying to screw both of us. (*He starts to tear up the expense sheet*)
Roger (*rising furiously*) Linda, I'm not staying here to be subjected to a vicious assault by a raving lunatic——(*He marches to the door with his briefcase and collects his overcoat*)
George Lunatic!

Roger marches DC

Roger (*to Linda*) And if he becomes violent ring me immediately.

Bernard enters from the kitchen during George's next line

George (*yelling*) And a Happy Christmas to you! (*He throws the pieces of paper into the air like snow*)
Bernard (*cheerfully*) Yes, Happy Christmas, Roger.
Roger Happy Christmas! (*Controlled*) I just want to say one thing to you, George—those old curtains of yours were bloody awful! (*He goes towards the front door*)

George surreptitiously squirts Roger's backside with soda

Roger stops and then makes a dignified exit

Bernard He's not upset about my sandwiches, is he?
Linda Sandwiches?
George The sandwiches were great!

Bernard moves above to George

Bernard Good. Because I was a bit worried about the Hurricane's Special Stuffing.

George marches away to the fireplace

George The Hurricane's Special Stuffing was great!
Bernard That's good too because I've just discovered that I put Gertie's dog food in the sandwiches instead of the stuffing.
George God almighty!
Linda (*rising*) I'm sure we had the stuffing, Bernard.
George (*to Bernard*) Why can't you let someone else make the bloody sandwiches?

Linda It's all right, Dad.
George (*pressing on, to Bernard*) Just stop interfering in everything!
Linda George! (*To Bernard*) It's not your fault, Dad. It's us.

George angrily collects the tray and moves towards kitchen as he speaks

George Well, he doesn't help matters. Under our feet all the time. Prattling on about Jock McIntosh and bloody Jumbo Phillpots. Who gives a damn about Jock McIntosh and bloody Jumbo Phillpots?
Linda George!

George storms into the kitchen with the tray

Bernard walks slowly upstairs

Dad . . .

Bernard stops and turns

Bernard You remember I got confused about George's vasectomy—I thought he'd had a lobotomy?
Linda Yes, Dad.
Bernard I reckon I was right the first time.

Bernard exits up the stairs

The front doorbell rings. Linda hesitates and then opens it

Betty enters carrying a bowl and a mixing spoon

Betty Roger's just come in like a madman. Everything all right?
Linda God knows!
Betty I thought you were going to have an amicable discussion.
Linda So did I. Drink?
Betty No thanks.
Linda I think I will. I need one. (*She moves to the drinks cabinet*)
Betty What on earth went wrong?
Linda I've really no idea.
Betty Did Roger try to cut your allowance out all together?
Linda No. He was very understanding. He thought one hundred and eighty-five a week was very fair.
Betty God, I'd move out for half that.

Linda sits at the L of the table with her drink

Linda Yes, George seems to think it was a bit much.

Betty sits on the R arm of the settee

Betty Linda—tell him to come back, you daft thing. You don't know when you're well off. Look what I have to put up with from Roger.
Linda Some of his jokes are quite amusing.
Betty I suppose Raquel could be classified as amusing.
Linda Raquel?
Betty Haven't you heard of the famous barmaid?

Linda No.

Betty That's possibly because you miss out on all the local gossip at the Golf Club. She's known there as the Great British Open.

Linda digests this

Linda What's this got to do with Roger?

Betty He's Raquel's handicap.

Linda You mean Roger and she——?

Betty Every Monday and Wednesday.

Linda I thought one of those was snooker and one poker.

Betty Well it transpires they're both poker.

Linda I see. Does he know you know?

Betty God, forbid, that'd ruin everything. No, Roger couldn't cope with the guilt. This way it works. For both of us. (*She rises*) Nothing's perfect, darling. Roger's oversexed—your George is a bit dull. Marriages may be made in heaven but they have to be lived in Woking.

George enters from the kitchen

George You might like to know that Dad didn't put dog food in the sandwiches, but he has stuffed several pounds of Pedigree Chum up the turkey's backside.

The girls react as George looks furious and gets himself a drink

Betty exits through the front door

Linda closes the front door and comes to sit on the L end of the settee

Linda You'll be sick.

George Good. (*He sits L of the table*)

Linda You won't be fit to drive the car.

George (*shrugging*) Get a taxi. (*He sips his drink*) It's dreadful, isn't it?

Linda What do you expect, all that whisky.

George No. After seventeen years together we sat here tonight negotiating like the Management and the Union.

Linda (*quietly*) I know.

George Is that all a marriage boils down to after all this time? How much do you spend on tablets? What does it cost to service the car? What's the price of a hair-do? Who gets the chair? Who gets the curtains? Who gets the dog?

Linda If I hadn't burnt your curtains you could have had them.

George Shall I tell you something? I'm glad you burnt them, I never liked them either.

Linda (*astonished*) You didn't?

George No. Hated them. I just didn't like to admit I'd made a mistake. (*He sips his drink*) It wasn't a bad marriage, Linda. It deserved a better ending than this.

Linda All we had was a secure, routine *existence*.

George I could have gone on like that for the rest of my life.

Linda Could you? Really?

George Oh yes.

Linda Well, I'm not ready to be put out to grass yet! (*She rises*) George, for the first time in years I've found myself looking forward to the day. It's exciting not knowing what's going to happen. My life has somewhere to go.

George I still don't see how I'm stopping it going.

There is a pause as Linda looks at him. Then she moves away

Linda Maybe it has more to do with our love life than I said. I wanted some romance. Some passion. I wanted to be grabbed hold of violently and made mad passionate love to. (*She looks straight at him*) And if my lover falls asleep on top of me I want it to be *after* not *during*!

There is a pause as they look at each other

Bernard comes downstairs wearing his RAF greatcoat and a muffler and hat. He moves to the front door

Bernard Just nipping out.

George rises and moves up to Bernard's R

George Dad, you don't have to go out.

Bernard I want to.

George I lost my temper. I'm sorry.

Bernard No call to apologize, son. It's your house.

George Dad, look, it's snowing. Please don't let's have any melodramatics, for God's sake.

Bernard I'm just popping down the road to the Club. Have a snifter or two. Cheer up the old codgers there. I'm right as ninepence, honestly.

Linda moves up to Bernard's L

Linda Well, wrap yourself up. (*She wraps his muffler round his neck*)

Bernard (*saluting*) Orders received, sir.

Linda And don't slip over.

Bernard Understood, sir.

Linda And don't forget, you're taking me to Betty and Roger's for punch, so be back by eight o'clock.

Bernard Twenty hundred hours, sir! And do you know something, George?

George What, Dad?

Bernard You were a bloody miserable baby, too.

Bernard exits through the front door

George considers Bernard's remark blankly for a moment

George He hardly ever *saw* me as a baby. That's probably what's wrong with me. Too much maternal influence. Poor old George Harper! All because of his mother. Introverted and undersexed. (*He sits on the R arm of the settee and lights his pipe*)

Linda All that drink's making you maudlin.

The telephone rings. Linda answers it

(*On the phone*) Hello? . . . (*Surprised*) Oh, hello! Fine thanks. . . . Tonight? Well, it's a bit short notice actually. . . . Oh, I see. (*She laughs*) All right then. . . . Fine. Oh, but we'll have to pop into Roger and Betty's on the way. . . . Yes. . . . OK. Eight o'clock sharp. Bye. (*She puts the phone down and comes to sit* R *of the table*)

George What was all that about?

Linda Nothing.

George Who's picking you up at eight o'clock sharp?

Linda Ken Robinson.

George Ken Robinson.

Linda You remember him. You played tennis with him. Tall, blond, looked a little bit like Robert Redford.

George Oh, yes! The Viking. Got a serve like a cannonball. And you've made a date with him?

Linda They're stuck. It's a Christmas Eve Dance. I'm just making up a foursome, that's all.

George (*rising*) That's a date!

Linda All right, if you want to call it a date, call it a date. Personally, I don't consider it a date and I think you're being a little ridiculous.

George I'm not being ridiculous, I'm being jealous. You told me a few minutes ago that you liked me being jealous.

Linda That's not being jealous, that's being irrational.

George I am not being irrational. I just don't want you going out with that virile Viking.

Linda George, you're forgetting. I can come and go as I please now.

George Yes, of course you can come and go as you please, but you're not going.

Linda And how do you propose to stop me?

For a moment George puffs furiously at his pipe, enveloped in smoke

George (*finally*) I'm going to make love to you!

Linda George——!

George pulls her up and around the table to C

George I'm going to make love to you like you've never had love made to you before. You want to be grabbed hold of and made mad, passionate love to? Right! We are going to have our rations!

Linda (*sarcastically*) Are we really? (*In one breath*) Well, Ken isn't picking me up until eight o'clock so if you intend to stop me by having sex then I suggest you don't start until a quarter to eight and if I know you I'll still be ready to go by eight o'clock sharp.

George Your little innuendos won't work this time, Linda. I'm going to give you what I should have given you when all this stupid separation talk started. I'm going to give you what you really want.

Linda Now, that's not going to suddenly make our marriage work.

George Maybe not, but it'll make your Awareness Group sit up!

He takes her towards the stairs but she stops

Linda Your father might come back!
George Great. I hope he brings Jock and Jumbo with him.
Linda George——
George When they see what I'm giving you, I'll get the Victoria Cross.

He pulls her towards the stairs as the telephone rings. They stop then George grabs it

> (*On the phone*) Hello! . . . Oh, hi, Ken, my old Viking. . . . Yes, surprise, it's George. . . . No you can't speak to my wife. . . . You want to tell her there's no need to dress? Don't worry, in ten seconds' time, she's going to be starkers. And you can forget about the date, she's being kept in, my old Viking.

Linda (*moving to George*) George!
George (*on the phone*) That's right, kept in. I'm going to give her double rations. (*He slams the phone down*)
Linda (*walking away*) You had no right to do that.
George Chocks away! Scramble!

George marches to Linda who halts him

Linda You've been drinking, George, and your behaviour's irrational.
George I'm going to have my irrationals!

Linda walks DL *and in front of the settee*

Linda (*moving but trying to be calm*) I know you don't mean it, George. It's not seven o'clock yet.
George So what! (*He starts to follow Linda*)
Linda You can never do anything before ten o'clock.
George Can't I?
Linda And then only if you've booked in advance.

George is now beside Linda below the settee

George Am I going to have my irrationals?
Linda No, you are not.

George turns Linda round

George Right! Linda, I'm going to have you because I've got to have you.

George kisses her passionately. She struggles for several seconds and then starts to complain while still being kissed

> (*Finally*) Don't speak with your mouth full.

He kisses her violently once more. After a few seconds Linda weakens and then pulls him closer. George comes out of the kiss, drops to his knees and hugs her round the waist

Linda (*breathless*) George, please——
George Let's go upstairs.

Linda No, let's do it here!
George On the rug in front of the fire?
Linda Yes, I'll get out of my clothes. Don't waste time with a coal fire, an electric one will do.

She rushes upstairs

George quickly removes his shoes and trousers

George Lights! Music! Action!

The doorbell rings. George freezes, then tries in vain to replace his trousers but finally throws them away. He buttons up his jacket and goes to the door

Who is it? Who is it?
Leonard (*from outside*) Leonard.
George Leonard isn't home. He went out.
Leonard (*from outside*) No, Dad, it's me, Leonard. Let me in.

Leonard opens the door and squeezes in a little

George What are you doing here?
Leonard I live here.
George That's not what I asked you. Answer the question. What are you doing here?
Leonard Geraldine and I had a row.
George Why did you have a row? I told you when you left here tonight to be nice to her. Now go back and apologize.
Leonard Dad, I can't go back and apologize to her—she's got another boy over there.
George Good, apologize to both of them.
Leonard I can't do that. I don't even know his name.
George This is no time to be shy, Leonard. Introduce yourself.
Leonard No, I can't Dad! (*Finally noticing*) What are you doing in your underpants?
George Your mother's teaching me some classes she learned in her yoga class.
Leonard Mum doesn't take yoga.
George No, but she's going to as soon as you get out of here.
Leonard (*realizing*) Ohhh! Hey! Good going, Dad!
George Go to the pictures, Leonard!
Leonard No, I'll got to Church and light a candle for you.

Leonard exits

George closes the door and starts to turn off the lights

Linda (*from upstairs*) Who was that?
George It was Leonard. He had the wrong house.
Linda (*from upstairs*) What?
George He forgot something. I gave it to him. (*To himself*) Now, where was I. Oh, yes. The fire. (*He arranges the electric fire in front of the fireplace*

*and turns it on—a red glow appears. He hurries over to the stereo and
searches through the records)*

*Linda rushes down the stairs. She has changed into a very provocative
négligé which has a cord tied round the middle. She pulls up short half-way
down the stairs and tries to walk down the remaining stairs in a lady-like
manner*

George moves DL *looking through records as Linda gets to* DC. *George sees her*

(*As he stares at her*) You look fantastic!
Linda So do you!
George What happned to all my Frank Sinatra records?
Linda I don't know, darling. Leonard's been using the record player.
George (*referring to a record sleeve*) Well, we can't make love to "Wham!",
I'll get a hernia. (*He replaces the records, looks at her again*) You look
fantastic. (*He approaches her above the settee*)
Linda So do you. You've put the fire on. (*She moves in front of the settee to*
DL)
George Yes.
Linda How about some nice candlelight?
George Good idea. Where are they?
Linda In the kitchen.
George I'll get them. I'll be right back.

He rushes to the kitchen

*Linda lies down in front of the sofa in preparation. After a moment she sits up
and puts the sofa cushions on the floor and lies down again*

George hurries back in

I can't find the candles. (*He looks around*) Where are you?
Linda On the floor.
George Oh. Lovely. God, you look fantastic. (*He excitedly moves towards
her*)
Linda So do you.
George Yes. Where are the candles?
Linda In the cupboard over the fridge.
George Right. I'll get them. I'll be right back. Don't start without me.

He rushes into the kitchen

*Linda lies down again. From the kitchen we hear a loud crash and barking.
Linda sits up*

Linda (*calling*) George! Are you all right?
George (*off*) I fell over the bloody dog.

*George limps in from the kitchen carrying two lighted candles. He comes
over to Linda*

Where are the candle holders?
Linda To hell with the candles!

She grabs the candles, blows them out, and throws them over her head. She pulls George down beside her and embraces him. George mumbles something

What are you mumbling, my darling?
George The music! I forgot to put on the music!
Linda We'll make our own music!

Linda pulls him back but he struggles up again

George It'll be better with music. I'll put on a long-playing record. This is going to be a long one, Linda! (*He rushes over to the stereo, and frantically searches through the records*)
Linda Any one will do, George.
George OK. (*He reads the sleeve*) "Selections From The Central Band of the Royal Air Force"?
Linda Perfect. Come on.

George puts the record on. After a moment the stereo blares out at a high volume "The Dam Busters March". George comes back to the sofa and kneels lovingly beside Linda. They look at each other. Suddenly Linda grabs him and pulls him on top of her. They kiss. Their breathing becomes heavier and their passion more intense. After a moment the record gets stuck. They ignore it for several seconds then George breaks the embrace and looks at the record player

Ignore it, George.
George All right. No, it'll worry me.

George hurries over to the stereo and hits it. The needle jumps and "Colonel Bogey" begins playing. George rushes back to Linda and falls on top of her. Suddenly the telephone rings. George rushes over to the telephone and lifts the receiver

(*On the phone*) Wrong number.

He bangs the receiver down. Linda gets up and turns off the stereo. George hurries back and flings himself on to the empty cushions. Linda hurries back to him. He kisses her all over

Linda (*frantic*) Kiss me, George. Kiss me.
George (*equally frantic*) I'm kissing you! I'm kissing you!
Linda Hold me, George! Hold me!
George I'm holding you! I'm holding you!
Linda (*more passionately*) Squeeze me, George, squeeze me!
George (*lifting his head up*) Will you stop telling me what to do when I'm doing it?!
Linda I'm sorry, darling.

George sits up against the settee

George God, it's so hot.
Linda I'll turn the fire off.

She crawls over to the fire, switches it off and crawls back again. George has sat up, some of his fervour gone

I want you George. Oo—I want you! (*She kisses him all over his chest*) I want you now! Now! George, please. Now! Now! (*She is trying to untie his tie and nearly strangles him*)

George (*desperately*) Bloody hell, it's just not working. The mood's gone.
Linda (*panting*) What do you mean, gone?

George sits up on the R end of the settee

George Well, what do you expect? What with the damn record player and the bloody telephone. With my hang-ups I need all the help I can get.

There is a pause

Linda (*hesitantly*) Would you like me to say rude things to you?
George Rude things?
Linda To get you going again.
George What sort of rude things?
Linda You know. Like—er—what I'd like you to do to me.
George (*shocked*) I've never heard you use that sort of language. No, I wouldn't like to hear you say those sort of—I don't know though. Yes! Tell me what you'd like me to do to you.

Linda kneels up on the L end of the settee

Linda Well—er . . .
George (*getting keen*) Yeah?
Linda I'd like you to—er . . .
George Yeah. Go on.
Linda I want a . . .
George (*excited*) I think it's going to work!
Linda I need a good . . .
George (*very excited*) Yes?!
Linda (*giving up*) It's no good, I can't say that word, George. (*She sits back into the settee*)
George Damn it, Linda, it was your idea.
Linda I know!
George Then if you want it, you'd better say it!
Linda (*conceding*) All right, George. I'll say it. I'll say it. I'll say it.
George (*half-crazed*) Stop saying you'll say it and *say* it, will you?!

Linda whispers in his ear

(*After a long pause*) What was that?
Linda I said it.
George I didn't hear it. You'll have to speak up.
Linda All right, I'll say it out loud. (*She takes a deep breath*) Do me!

George looks at her blankly

George I beg your pardon.
Linda Do me!
George *Do* you? That's not the word I want to hear. Say the *other* word.

Linda Oh, I couldn't, George, I just couldn't. (*Suddenly*) I'll write it down for you!
George (*frustrated*) OK, OK. Write it down. Anything!

She grabs a pencil and pad from beside the stereo and starts scribbling

And print it. You know I can't read your handwriting.

George takes out a pair of reading glasses as Linda hands George the piece of paper and lies down. George reads it and his eyes open wide

(*On fire*) Oh, my God!

George grabs her and starts to kiss her on the neck while fumbling madly with the cord around the middle of her négligé

Linda Hurry, sweetheart, hurry.
George I can't get the damn thing undone.

They struggle together

Linda Rip it, George, rip it!
George I'm trying to rip it!

> *The kitchen door bursts open and Gertie rushes in barking. She runs over to George and Linda and playfully joins in the "fun". Linda and George get up and take Gertie to the door*

Linda Come on, Gertie. Tinkles! (*She opens the front door*)

> *A choir of Carol Singers are revealed, singing "Hark! The Herald Angels Sing". Gertie exits*

Linda rushes round to hide below the settee. George picks up his trousers and starts to search through the pockets. He gives up and flings the trousers at the Carol Singers, and slams the door. He hurries back to Linda who is still attempting to rip her cord

George I'll do it!
Linda I'm doing it!
George You've put a knot in it! Turn over!

Linda gets on her tummy, and George tries to break the cord by pulling it up from the middle whilst standing on the sofa. The cord breaks and he goes flying backwards over the sofa

Linda George!

Linda stands on the sofa to look over as George's head appears

George (*slightly dazed*) I'm all right.
Linda Oh, George darling. Darling, George.

Linda bends to kiss him. They go into a warm embrace during which they murmur "sweet nothings" while George gently takes her down over the back of the sofa. The sound of the "sweet nothings" continue

Then Roger flies into the room through the front door. He turns the lights on, and reacts to what he sees going on behind the sofa

Roger You bloody swine!

Roger goes to the bar, grabs the soda syphon and sprays them with it. He then pulls up a speechless Linda from behind the sofa

(*To Linda*) Don't worry. It's all right. Everything's fine. Forget all about it. You're safe now. There there. Roger's here. Good old Uncle Roger. No problems.

Linda (*quietly*) Roger, do you know what you are?

Roger No need to thank me. Just grateful I rang up to see if you were all right. When George said "wrong number" and left the phone off the hook I knew what was in his filthy mind. You can have him in court for that.

Linda We were just about to settle out of court.

Roger Oh no!

George sits up from behind the sofa. He is soaking wet from the soda. He crosses in front of Linda to Roger

George You know what you are, don't you?

Roger Yes. I think I do.

Linda It's all right darling. Maybe we don't need Roger's help any more.

George (*smiling broadly*) Don't we?

Linda No.

She kisses George and they embrace

Roger Well, I can see I'm not needed. Jolly good. See you, George, Linda. Yes, well, I think I'd better——

George breaks the embrace to whisper something short and sharp in Roger's ear and then returns to the embrace

    Roger hurries out through the front door

After a moment George and Linda break their embrace

George It still won't be easy, you know.

Linda Probably not.

George I expect I'll always be a bit of a stick-in-the-mud.

Linda Probably.

George And you'll always be hankering after a bit more excitement.

Linda Probably. But I expect that'll gradually diminish as I get past forty.

They kiss. Linda breaks it

I think there's too much traffic in the living-room don't you?

George Definitely!

As they move to go upstairs

    Bernard enters through the front door with Gertie

Bernard I ask you! They close the Club on Christmas Eve. (*To George*) Are you still here?

Linda Yes, Dad. We're going to bed.

Bernard (*surprised*) Bed? What about Christmas punch next door?

Linda We'll be up in time for that.

Bernard Well, what on earth are you going to bed for?

George Come on, Dad, your memory can't be as bad as all that.

George and Linda go upstairs. Gertie follows them

Bernard chuckles as——

the CURTAIN slowly falls

FURNITURE AND PROPERTY LIST

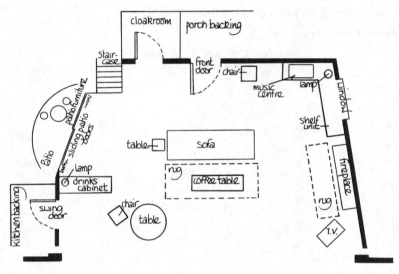

ACT I

SCENE 1

On stage: Fireplace. *In grate:* coal fire. *At side of fireplace:* electric fire, fireguard
Mantelpiece. *On it:* vase of flowers
TV. *On wall above it:* framed wedding photograph of George and Linda
Sofa. *On it:* cushions, potato crisps for **Bernard**
Small table
Coffee table. *On it:* ashtray, drinks mats
Larger table. *On it:* cloth, ashtray
Chair with arms
Drinks cabinet. *On it:* telephone, table lamp, dog-lead. *In it:* glasses,
    bottles of whisky, brandy, Perrier water
Shelf unit. *On it:* music centre, table lamp. *On shelves:* records
Upright chair
Carpet
Hearthrug, rug in front of sofa
On walls: mirror DR, pictures
In cloakroom: **Bernard**'s scarf and coat
Curtains at patio windows (open)
Blind at small window (closed)
Garden furniture on patio

Off stage: Basket of oranges **(Betty)**
Tray with 4 mugs of tea **(Linda** or **Betty)**
2 toasted sandwiches on plates **(Bernard)**
Pyjama jacket **(George)**

Personal: **George:** wedding ring (required throughout), pipe, matches, wrist-watch
Linda: wedding ring (required throughout)

SCENE 2

Strike: Tray, mugs, plates, remains of sandwiches, dirty glasses
Record from music centre

Set: Window curtains open
Linda's handbag containing handkerchief on coffee table

Check: **Linda's** coat in cloakroom

Off stage: Briefcase, umbrella **(George)**
Football **(Leonard)**
Ice-bag **(Linda)**

Personal: **Linda:** ear-rings
George: wrist-watch, 2 rings in boxes in pocket

SCENE 3

Strike: Dirty glasses, briefcase, umbrella, ice-bag, rings and boxes

Set: Patio doors open
Window curtains open
Blind at small window open
Wheelbarrow full of weeds and bush prunings
Tray of snacks on coffee table

Off stage: Glass of fizzing Alka Seltzer **(George)**
Rake **(Bernard)**
2 bags of groceries **(Linda)**
Piece of greenery plus root **(Bernard)**
Wheelbarrow containing Bernard **(Roger)**

Personal: **Roger:** £5 note in pocket

ACT II

Strike: Dirty glasses, wheelbarrow
Gaudy curtains
Lampshades
Cushions from sofa
Cloth, ashtray from larger table
Hearthrug, rug in front of sofa
Coffee table
Wedding photo
Garden furniture from patio

Set: New curtains at patio windows (curtains open)
New lampshades

New cushions on sofa
New hearthrug, new rug in front of sofa
Beginner's oil painting on wall above TV
Sculpture, 2 expenses folders, decanter of whisky, soda syphon, vase of
    flowers on drinks cabinet
Christmas tree with lights, decorations and presents
Christmas cards and decorations around room
Box of decorations
Pair of step ladders
Notepad and pencil by music centre
Leonard's shoes by fireplace
Leonard's skiing jacket in cloakroom
Fireguard over coal fire in fireplace
Electric fire pulled out
Small window blind closed
Snow on patio
Fresh flowers in vase on mantelpiece
Record on music centre turntable

Off stage: Wrapped Christmas presents **(Betty)**
Wrapped Christmas presents **(George)**
Christmas decoration **(Leonard)**
Briefcase containing papers, pen **(Roger)**
Carrier bag containing football boots, annual **(Linda)**
Mugs of coffee **(Roger)**
Tray with mugs of coffee and sandwiches **(Roger)**
Bowl, mixing spoon **(Betty)**
2 lighted candles **(George)**

Personal: **Betty:** snow
Bernard: sprig of mistletoe in pocket
George: snow, wrist-watch, pipe, tobacco, matches, spectacles in pocket
Roger: snow
Bernard: false beard, small Father Christmas hat in pocket
Roger: small Father Christmas hat

LIGHTING PLOT

Practical fittings required: 2 table lamps, wall-brackets, TV effect, coal fire effect, electric fire effect, Christmas tree lights, patio lights

Interior. A living-room. The same scene throughout

ACT I, Scene 1 Evening

To open: Dim interior lighting—table lamps on, TV effect on, smouldering coal fire effect on

Cue 1	**George** enters and switches on main lights *Snap on wall-brackets*	(Page 2)
Cue 2	**Linda** switches off TV *Cut TV effect*	(Page 2)
Cue 3	**George** switches off wall-brackets and table lamps *Snap off wall-brackets and table lamps*	(Page 15)
Cue 4	**Linda** (*off*): "George?" (*3rd time*) *Black-out*	(Page 15)

ACT I, Scene 2 Early evening

To open: Table lamps on

Cue 5	**George** follows **Bernard** out, closing the door *Black-out*	(Page 27)

ACT I, Scene 3 Noon

To open: General interior lighting, winter sunshine streaming in through windows, flickering coal fire effect on, TV effect on

Cue 6	**George** switches off TV *Cut TV effect*	(Page 28)
Cue 7	**Leonard** switches on TV *Bring up TV effect*	(Page 29)
Cue 8	**Linda** switches off TV *Cut TV effect*	(Page 31)

ACT II Early evening

To open: Dim interior lighting—table lamps on, Christmas tree lights on, patio lights on

Cue 9	**Leonard** switches on main lights *Snap on wall-brackets*	(Page 38)

Cue 10   **George** switches off main lights   (Page 61)
          Snap off wall-brackets

Cue 11   **George** switches on electric fire   (Page 62)
          Snap up electric fire effect

Cue 12   **Linda** crawls over to fire and switches it off   (Page 63)
          Cut electric fire effect

Cue 13   **Roger** flies into room and switches on main lights   (Page 66)
          Snap on wall-brackets

EFFECTS PLOT

ACT I

Cue 1   As CURTAIN rises   (Page 1)
          Sound from TV—James Cagney film

Cue 2   **George** turns down volume on TV   (Page 2)
          Decrease sound from TV

Cue 3   **Linda** switches off TV   (Page 2)
          Cut TV sound

Cue 4   **Linda:** "Nonsense".   (Page 3)
          Loud smoochy mood music from music centre

Cue 5   **Linda** turns down volume   (Page 3)
          Decrease music

Cue 6   **George** turns off music centre   (Page 6)
          Cut music

Cue 7   **Linda:** "And the dog."   (Page 17)
          Telephone rings

Cue 8   As Scene 3 opens   (Page 28)
          Sound from TV—football match coverage

Cue 9   **George** switches off TV   (Page 28)
          Cut TV sound

Cue 10 **Leonard** turns up sound on TV   (Page 30)
          Bring up TV sound

Cue 11 **Linda** switches off TV   (Page 31)
          Snap off TV sound

ACT II

Cue 12 As Act opens   (Page 38)
          Loud rock music from music centre; snow falling outside on patio—continue throughout

Cue 13 **Leonard** switches off record   (Page 38)
          Cut music

Cue 14 As **Leonard** and **Bernard** start upstairs   (Page 40)
          Front doorbell

Cue 15 **Leonard** and **George** shake hands   (Page 43)
          Front doorbell

Cue 16 **Bernard** exits up the stairs   (Page 56)
          Front doorbell

Cue 17   **Linda:** ". . . making you maudlin."   (Page 58)
          Telephone rings

Cue 18   **George:** ". . . I'll get the Victoria Cross."   (Page 60)
          Telephone rings

Cue 19   **George:** "Lights! Music! Action!"   (Page 61)
          Front doorbell

Cue 20   **George** rushes into kitchen; **Linda** lies down again   (Page 62)
          Loud crash and barking from kitchen, off

Cue 21   **George** puts record on music centre   (Page 63)
          Loud music: "The Dam Busters March"

Cue 22   As **George** and **Linda** become very passionate   (Page 63)
          Record sticks

Cue 23   **George** hits music centre   (Page 63)
          Needle jumps, then "Colonel Bogey" plays

Cue 24   **George** rushes back to **Linda** and falls on top of her   (Page 63)
          Telephone rings

Cue 25   **Linda** gets up and turns off record   (Page 63)
          Cut music

MADE AND PRINTED IN GREAT BRITAIN BY
LATIMER TREND & COMPANY LTD PLYMOUTH
MADE IN ENGLAND